THE MINDÛP CURRICULUM

CURRICULUM

Grades Pre-K–2

Focused Classrooms • Mindful Learning • Resilient Students

SCHOLASTIC

•••

Acknowledgments

With heartfelt appreciation to Goldie Hawn, Founder of The Hawn Foundation, for her vision, commitment, compassion, and dedicated advocacy for children everywhere.

We would like to thank the many scientists, researchers, and educators who contributed to the MindUP curriculum.

Pat Achtyl; Thelma Anselmi; Angie Balius; Lorraine Bayne; Michelle Beaulieu; Peter Canoll, MD, PhD; Beck Collie; Adele Diamond, PhD; Diane Dillon, PhD; Jennifer Erickson; Nancy Etcoff, PhD; Pam Hoeffner; Nicole Iorio; Greg Jabaut; Ann Kelly; Molly Stewart Lawlor; Noreen Maguire; Marc A. Meyer, PhD; Cindy Middendorf; Christine Boardman Moen; Tammy Murphy, PhD; Charlene Myklebust, PhD; Nicole Obadia; Carol B. Olson, PhD; Janice Parry; Lisa Pedrini; Tina Posner; Kimberly Schonert-Reichl, PhD; Patti Vitale; Judy Willis, MD, MEd; Victoria Zelenak

•••

ISBN-10: 0-545-26712-9
ISBN-13: 978-0-545-26712-0

19 20   40   19 18

Table of Contents

Welcome to MINDUP

Imagine … joyful learning, academic success, and a powerful sense of self and community.

Imagine … students who are able to engage in a focused, energetic way with one another, with their teachers, and with their learning.

Imagine … schools that are productive, harmonious centers of successful learning, where all students thrive because they recognize themselves as

- capable, creative learners
- self-aware human beings
- compassionate, responsible citizens

All of this is possible. **MINDUP** can help you achieve it.

MindUP Online Training

At **www.thehawnfoundation.org**, you'll find resources to enrich your MindUP instruction, including
- the entire spectrum of MindUP techniques, addressing social and emotional learning
- classroom demonstrations conducted by experienced MindUP consultants and mentors
- instructional insights, grade-specific teaching strategies, and other resources
- the latest in neuroscience about how the brain works and how it affects learning

Register at **www.thehawnfoundation.org** to access this innovative, interactive training and learning resource, developed in partnership with Columbia University's Center for New Media Teaching and Learning.

Dear Educators,

From Scholastic

For 90 years, Scholastic has been a presence in your classrooms, supporting teaching and learning. The challenges faced by you and your students today are well known and unprecedented. These include the following expectations:

- providing differentiated instruction to children who come with diverse language and experiential backgrounds
- improving academic performance
- addressing new standards geared to career and college preparedness
- helping children and their families handle economic and social changes

When we met Goldie Hawn and the Hawn Foundation team, we were impressed by their commitment to helping all students achieve their potential socially and academically. Also, we shared their respect for educators who, like all of you, are entrusted with the preparation of the next generation.

We are pleased to introduce MindUP, a collaboration of the Hawn Foundation and Scholastic. MindUP isn't one more program to implement or subject to teach, but a set of strategies that can be integrated with what you are already doing, so that you and your students will become more focused when doing schoolwork and are able to work and play more successfully with others. The essence of what the MindUP program calls for is embodied in the idea of the Optimistic Classroom—a place where all children have the opportunity to achieve their potential.

Thank you for inviting us into your school.

Optimistically yours,

Francie Alexander *Patrick Daley*

Francie Alexander
Chief Academic Officer
Scholastic Inc.

Patrick Daley
Senior Vice President, Publisher
Scholastic Inc.

From the Hawn Foundation

Thank you for bringing the MindUP Curriculum into your classrooms.

MindUP has been my focus and my passion for many years. I am so grateful to you, devoted educators who believe in the limitless potential of children and give tirelessly of your time, energy, creativity, and love.

The simple practices at the core of MindUP will help your students to become resilient, focused, and mindful learners. I have seen the MindUP practices at work in classrooms all over the world. I have witnessed its success and have heard from countless teachers in praise of its transformative effect on children's ability to learn.

I know that with your help we can equip our children with the skills they need to live smarter, healthier, and happier lives. Together we will create optimistic classrooms where children successfully cope with the stresses they face in school, at home, and in their communities.

Thank you for accepting the enormous and critically important responsibilities and challenges that accompany your mission as an educator.

From the bottom of my heart, I thank you.

Goldie Hawn

Goldie Hawn
Founder, The Hawn Foundation
and the MindUP Curriculum

What is MindUP?

MindUP is a comprehensive, classroom-tested, evidence-based curriculum framed around 15 easily implemented lessons that foster social and emotional awareness, enhance psychological well-being, and promote academic success.

The MindUP classroom is an optimistic classroom that promotes and develops mindful attention to oneself and others, tolerance of differences, and the capacity of each member of the community to grow as a human being and a learner. MindUP's expansive dynamic is built to a large extent on routine practices that are inherent to the MindUP Curriculum. Over the course of the MindUP experience, children learn about the brain and how it functions, in the process gaining insight into their own minds and behaviors as well as those of the people around them.

How Does MindUP Work?

The essential work of MindUP is accomplished through the lessons themselves, which include the repetition of the Core Practice—deep belly breathing and attentive listening. The Core Practice makes mindful attention the foundation for learning and interacting; ideally, it is repeated for a few moments of each school day throughout the year. (See Lesson 3, page 42, for a complete overview of the Core Practice.)

> "MindUP makes my brain happy,
> so I can learn better."
> —David, first grade

MindUP has the capacity to alter the landscape of your classroom by letting children in on the workings of their own agile minds. Each MindUP lesson begins with background information on the brain, introducing a specific area of concentration with an activity in which children can see concrete examples of how their brain functions. As you and your clas become accustomed to learning about the ways in which the brain processes information, your students will become habitually more observant of their own learning process.

MindUP offers teachers and children insights that respond to the natural thoughtfulness of young people and lead to self-regulation of their behavior. MindUP is dedicated to the belief that the child who learns to monitor his or her senses and feelings becomes more aware and better understands how to respond to the world *reflectively* instead of *reflexively*.

Who Needs MindUP?

Everyone. Joyful engagement isn't incidental; it's essential. Yet, young people today are no strangers to stress. From an early age, they experience stress from a range of sources. For some, stress goes hand in hand with the pressure to achieve; for others, it is prompted by economic hardship, poor nutrition, or inadequate health care; for still others, it may be linked to emotional deprivation or limited educational resources. Whatever the particular circumstance, any one of these factors could hamper a child's ability to learn without anxiety. In "communities of turmoil" (Tatum, 2009), children often cope with several problems at once, and suffer from chronic stress—with consequences that can be disastrous for their learning and their lives. MindUP addresses these obstacles to productive learning and living by offering children and teachers simple practices and insights that become tools for self-management and self-possession. At the same time, the MindUP program works to make learning joyful and fun by emphasizing learning modes in which children flourish:

- lively instruction that invites problem solving, discussion, and exploration
- teacher modeling and coaching
- cross-age mentoring and decision making among children
- conflict resolution
- inquiry and the arts

Joyful engagement is not incidental; it's essential. MindUP shows you how to put joy into your teaching.

The Research Base

Broadly defined, mindful attention centers on conscious awareness of the present moment: by focusing our attention and controlling our breath, we can learn to reduce stress and optimize the learning capacity of the brain. The use of these practices in MindUP is informed by leading-edge research in the fields of developmental cognitive neuroscience, mindfulness training, social and emotional learning (SEL), and positive psychology. In particular, MindUP pursues objectives roughly parallel to those of the five-point framework of competencies laid out in the work of the Collaborative for Academic, Social, and Emotional Learning (CASEL; www.casel.org), a not-for-profit organization at the forefront in efforts to advance the science- and evidence-based practice of social and emotional learning (SEL). These areas of competency are:

Self-Awareness
Assessing our feelings, interests, values, and strengths; maintaining self-confidence.

Self-Management
Regulating emotions to handle stress, control impulses, and persevere in overcoming obstacles

Social Awareness
Understanding different perspectives and empathizing with others; recognizing and appreciating similarities and differences; using family, school, and community resources effectively

Relationship Skills
Maintaining healthy relationships based on cooperation; resisting inappropriate social pressure; preventing, managing, and resolving interpersonal conflicts; seeking help when needed

Responsible Decision Making
Using a variety of considerations, including ethical, academic, and community-related standards to make choices and decisions

Social and Emotional Learning

It is now well established that social and emotional skills, such as the ability to manage one's emotions and get along with others, play an integral role in academic and life success. Evidence supporting this statement is illustrated in several recent studies. Durlak et al. (2011) conducted a meta-analysis of 213 school-based, universal social and emotional learning (SEL) programs involving 270,034 students from kindergarten through high school and found that, compared to students not exposed to SEL classroom-based programming, students in SEL programs demonstrated significantly improved social and emotional skills, attitudes, behavior, and academic performance that reflected an 11-percentile-point gain in achievement. The importance of SEL in predicting school success has been further demonstrated by Caprara et al. (2000), who found that changes in academic achievement in grade 8 could be better predicted from knowing children's social competence five years earlier than from grade 3 academic competence. As Daniel Goleman, widely recognized as the "founding father" of emotional intelligence (EI), notes, these "remarkable results" make it clear that SEL has "delivered on its promise" (2008).

Adele Diamond, neuroscientist and founder of developmental cognitive neuroscience, found that students who learn SEL techniques such as role-playing consistently score higher on tests requiring use of the brain's executive functions—coordinating and controlling, monitoring and troubleshooting, reasoning and imagining (2007). Similarly, research conducted by social-emotional development expert Kimberly Schonert-Reichl found that "as predicted . . . at posttest teachers in the intervention classrooms described their students as significantly more attentive, emotionally regulated, and socially and emotionally competent than did teachers in the control classrooms" (2010).

As all teachers know, bored children often get into mischief; engaged ones are less likely to act out. Sadly, too often, what students enjoy most is what they get to do the least: discuss, debate, explore the arts, and participate in drama and group research projects. As research demonstrates, "Students experienced a greater level of understanding of concepts and ideas when they talked, explained, and argued about them with their group instead of just passively listening to a lecture or reading a test" (Iidaka et al., 2000). When education is fun, and students are engaged, focused, and inspired to participate, learning flourishes.

SEL programs such as MindUP also significantly impart to students a the sense of hopefulness.

> Hope changes brain chemistry, which influences the decisions we make and the actions we take. Hopefulness must be pervasive and every single student should be able to feel it, see it, and hear it daily (Jensen, 2009; p. 112–113).

Being hopeful mirrors physical activity; both physical activity and hopefulness enhance metabolic states and influence brain-changing gene expression (Jiaxu and Weiyi, 2000). Hope and optimism enable achievement. Hopeful kids are more likely to work diligently and not to give up or drop out—they work harder, persevere longer, and ultimately experience success, which in turn begets more success. It is a simple but profound and life-transforming cycle (Dweck, 2006)—one that is conscientiously cultivated in the MindUP classroom.

. . . .

The Stressed Brain

The brain's response to stress is linked to the function of the amygdala (uh-MIG-duh-luh), a small, almond-shaped clump of neurons deep in the center of our brain. The amygdala serves as an information filter regulated by our emotional state. When we're calm and peaceful, the filter is wide open and information flows to the prefrontal cortex, where the brain's so-called executive functions take place.

On the other hand, when we are feeling negative and stressed out, these executive functions, which provide cognitive control, are inhibited. Indeed, information stays in the amygdala; it doesn't flow into the prefrontal cortex for executive processing. Instead, it's processed right on the spot as fight, flight, or freeze. In this way, fear and anxiety effectively shut down higher-order thinking. Your impulse to flee a falling branch, or to defend yourself against physical assault, is an example of your body not bothering to "think about" what to do—you react without thinking.

Eric Jensen, veteran educator and brain expert, in *Teaching With Poverty in Mind: What Being Poor Does to Kids' Brains and What Schools Can Do About It* (2009) has this to say about stress and its effect on the brain:

> The biology of stress is simple in some ways and complex in others. On a basic level, every one of the 30–50 trillion cells in your body is experiencing either healthy or unhealthy growth. Cells cannot grow and deteriorate at the same time. Ideally, the body is in homeostatic balance: a state in which the vital measures of human function—heart rate, blood pressure, blood sugar, and so on—are in their optimal ranges. A stressor is anything that threatens to disrupt homeostasis—for example, criticism, neglect, social exclusion, lack of enrichment, malnutrition, drug use, exposure to toxins, abuse, or trauma. When cells aren't growing, they're in a "hunker down" mode that conserves resources for a threatened future. When billions or trillions of cells are under siege in this manner, you get problems (p. 23).

Neurobiological studies of neglected or abused children have revealed alarming alterations in brain development. The "fight, flight, or freeze" stress hormones that our bodies produce in response to physical and emotional adversity "atrophy the areas that control emotional development" (p. 25).

• •

The Happy Brain

To paraphrase Adele Diamond: Happy brains work better (2009).

When we're happy and engaged in activities that we find pleasurable (everything from painting to playing), our brain is flush with dopamine, a neurotransmitter that also helps lubricate our information filter and rev up high-powered thinking in our prefrontal cortex. Dopamine helps get our brains ready for peak performance. Indeed, just the anticipation of pleasurable learning stimulates dopamine flow.

The dopamine pleasure surge is highest when students are fully engaged with their learning and brimming with positive feelings such as optimism, gratitude, hope, and an overall sense of well-being. Classroom activities that give rise to the pleasure surge and prompt the release of dopamine include:

- participating in acts of kindness
- collaborating with peers
- making choices and solving problems
- engaging in physical activities such as sports, dance, and play
- enjoying creative efforts and disciplines such as music, art, drama, reading, and storytelling

Of course, dopamine is also released when people indulge in high-risk activities such as drug or alcohol use, promiscuity, fast driving, and overeating. However, when kids get their pleasure surge from activities that generate positive feelings overall, they are less likely to seek it in high-risk activities that also promote dopamine release (Galvan, et al., 2006; Kann, et al., 2006).

The Mindful Brain

MindUP is dedicated to helping children deepen their understanding of their own mental processes; the curriculum begins with an introduction to brain physiology. Once students become familiar with the parts of the brain and with how the parts function and interact, they carry that knowledge forward into their MindUP explorations as well as the rest of their classroom experience. The recommended daily Core Practice and the content of each lesson serve as conduits through which young learners can broaden their awareness of the connections between brain and body, between what goes on "inside" and actual experience. The outcome of this enhanced awareness is a group of resilient children whose awareness of their impulses, thoughts, feelings, and behavior enhances their confidence, pleasure, and sense of agency in their own learning process.

Consider the benefits that MindUP makes possible! Mindful teaching and learning:

- improve children's self-control and self-regulation skills
- strengthen children's resiliency and decision making
- bolster children's enthusiasm for learning
- increase students' academic success
- reduce peer-to-peer conflict
- develop children's positive social skills, such as empathy, compassion, patience, and generosity
- infuse your classroom learning with joy and optimism

MindUP and the School Day

The MindUP program was developed not only to expand children's social and emotional awareness but also to improve their academic performance. The concepts and vocabulary associated with MindUP will expand the scope of students' thinking in all academic disciplines.

MindUP Core Practice can become a staple routine for the opening and closing of each school day as well as at the moments of transition: settling down after recess, waiting for lunch, moving from one subject to the next. As countless MindUP teachers have discovered, any topic benefits from being approached with focused awareness.

The MindUP lessons themselves can be worked smoothly into a daily routine and require minimal preparation on your part; suggested follow-up activities link each lesson to content-area learning. You'll likely find yourself adopting the MindUP techniques and strategies across subject areas. MindUP may well become a way of life for you and the children in your class!

The Day Begins

The best teachers we know are mindful about the beginning of each school day. They make a point of standing by the school door and greeting with an open heart and welcoming smile every child who passes through their classroom door.

An ideal way to unify the class as they begin their day is to gather and share a few moments of "checking in," followed by the Core Practice of deep breathing and mindful awareness. Once you have established this simple routine, you will find that the day feels more coherent and the group less scattered as this practice brings the group together organically while setting an easygoing tone for engagement with the rest of your daily learning.

Transitions

The MindUP Core Practice works beautifully during transition times. With your guidance and thoughtful attention, you can accustom your children to respond to a simple reminder at which they habitually turn to the Core Practices to center themselves and prepare to move easily— even eagerly and joyfully—to the next classroom activity. "Our classroom transition times are some of the most important routines of our day....Our days are full, our curriculum is rich, and we have so much to do together! The tighter our transitions, the more time we will have for instruction" (Allyn, 2010).

The Day Ends

Just as you can help students greet a new day with eagerness and mindful purpose, so can you close the day with a spirit of purpose and celebration—your students will leave the classroom feeling calm yet energized. Eric Jensen, whose "brain-based" teaching has transformed teaching and learning in countless classrooms, explains, "Asking kids to visualize success on an upcoming skill or knowledge set is no 'new Age' strategy. When done well, mental practice is known not only to make physical changes in the brain but also to improve task performance (Pascual-Leone et al., 2005)" (2010). The goal is to end the day on a high note.

Breathing First: The Core Practice

From the earliest grades on up, the recommended approach to
MindUP is to first establish the habit of deep belly breathing and
focused attention—the so-called Core Practice. Well before you
teach Lesson 1, you can lay the groundwork for it in your class by
introducing the Core Practice in the first days of the school year.
Once children have learned the simple techniques of breathing and
listening, you will be able to use the Core Practice to unify your
classroom community and provide the stability and receptivity
needed for days of rich and fruitful learning. (See Lesson 3, page 42,
for a full explanation of the practice.)

Literacy expert Pam Allyn
has visited and observed
hundreds of classrooms
around the world.
"We have seen many
classrooms where there
are lots of pieces in place,
but one secret, fabulous
ingredient is missing. That
ingredient is celebration.
We see teachers wait to
celebrate until the end
of the year, until a child
does well on a test, until
the child actually masters
the art of reading. But
why wait? Celebration is
the ultimate management
strategy.... It is the core
ingredient that infuses
the entire life of the
classroom with joy,
with hope, with faith,
and with optimism"
(2010, p.107).

Using MindUP in the Classroom

MindUP comprises 15 lessons arranged into four units:

> **Unit I: Getting Focused (Lessons 1–3)**
> Introduce brain physiology and the concept of mindful attention; establish daily Core Practice
> **Lessons:** 1. How Our Brains Work, 2. Mindful Awareness, 3. Focused Awareness: The Core Practice
>
> **Unit II: Sharpening Your Senses (Lessons 4–9)**
> Experience the relationship between our senses, our moving bodies, and the way we think
> **Lessons:** 4. Mindful Listening, 5. Mindful Seeing, 6. Mindful Smelling, 7. Mindful Tasting, 8. Mindful Movement I, 9. Mindful Movement II
>
> **Unit III: It's All About Attitude (Lessons 10–12)**
> Understand the role of our mind-set in how we learn and progress
> **Lessons:** 10. Perspective Taking, 11. Choosing Optimism, 12. Appreciating Happy Experiences
>
> **Unit IV: Taking Action Mindfully (Lessons 13–15)**
> Apply mindful behaviors to our interactions with our community and the world
> **Lessons:** 13. Expressing Gratitude, 14. Performing Acts of Kindness, 15. Taking Mindful Action in the World

The framework is designed to strengthen children's sense of social and emotional well-being while creating a cohesive, caring classroom environment. Because the concepts build on one another, you'll find it most productive to teach the lessons in sequential order.

Lesson Structure

Each lesson follows the same format:

Introduction to the Lesson Topic... identifies and explains the subject of the lesson, frames *why* it's important, and includes testimony from a MindUP teacher.

Linking to Brain Research... explains how each lesson relates to the neuroscience. This section provides background for you, some of which you may want to share with your students to help them gain a progressively more sophisticated awareness of how their brains work.

Clarify for the Class... includes guidelines for making brain research concepts accessible to students at various grade levels.

Getting Ready... identifies what the lesson entails as well as learning goals for the lesson. Also listed are materials and resources required for leading the lesson.

MindUP Warm-Up... helps the class prepare for the Engage, Explore, Reflect part of the lesson activity by introducing and discussing subject matter in an easygoing, open-ended way that relates content to children's lives.

Leading the Lesson... offers a step-by-step approach that engages children in the inquiry, helps them explore the topic, and encourages them to reflect upon and discuss their insights and experiences. The lesson layout also establishes concrete links to the learning process and classroom issues at the Pre-K through second grade levels.

Connecting to the Curriculum... offers specific opportunities for children to bend their minds around language arts, math, social studies, science, health, physical education, the arts, and social-emotional learning. These optional across-the-curriculum learning experiences expand the lesson and offer alternative approaches to content.

Special Features

Creating the Optimistic Classroom... offers classroom management strategies for reaching English language learners, special needs students, and general learners in order to maximize the effectiveness of the lesson.

MindUP in the Real World... connects lesson content to a career or undertaking, expands discussion beyond the classroom, and grounds ideas in a concrete application.

Once a Day... suggests ways for teachers to apply lesson content to everyday situations involving children or colleagues.

Journal Writing... gives children an opportunity to reflect on motivation, actions, and their consequences, so they can learn to mediate and understand their actions. According to Susan Kaiser Greenland, journaling allows children to use what they've learned to create happier, more successful lives for themselves (2010). We recommend that you provide children with a notebook to create a journal that they can personalize with decorations of their choice, and use this personal record to document responses within Greenland's general framework of

- What I Noticed
- What It Means
- What I Learned

For the youngest learners, set up a Visual Journal for them to record responses with drawings and early efforts at handwriting.

Literature Link... recommends four books that extend the learning.

Lesson Opener

Each MindUP lesson is focused on one aspect or practice of the curriculum.

The targeted curriculum area is defined and placed in context for the teacher.

Experience of MindUP users attests to the effectiveness of the specific practice or lesson.

Brain research related to lesson exploration is laid out for instructor, along with supporting illustration.

Language and modeling help instructor make the brain research link understandable to students.

Getting Ready

This two-page spread offers an opportunity for easing into the main lesson, so that students are most receptive to the language and ideas that follow.

The core lesson ties in with wider self-management and awareness skills. Materials used are basic and usually already available in the classroom or as reproducible pages.

Before each core lesson, a simple preparatory activity helps both teacher and student know what to expect from the lesson and think in advance about how it may be useful in a broader context of learning.

Suggestions for classroom management, supporting brain-based learning, and helping all learners address common obstacles to attentiveness and full engagement with learning.

Leading the Lesson

Lessons are supported by findings of educators and researchers on the effectiveness of mindful awareness strategies.

Each lesson routine includes an introduction with scripting to prime children for the exploration and perspective at the core of the teaching.

Core activity of each lesson includes suggested language and procedures to maximize student absorption of the ideas and experience.

At each stage of the lesson, we point out the usefulness of the activity or provide a link to other curriculum areas in which lesson ideas can be implemented.

Lesson focus is extended into its application in the workplace, encouraging students to link learning to the world outside the classroom.

Suggestions for the teacher to incorporate mindful awareness into his or her everyday interactions with colleagues and students.

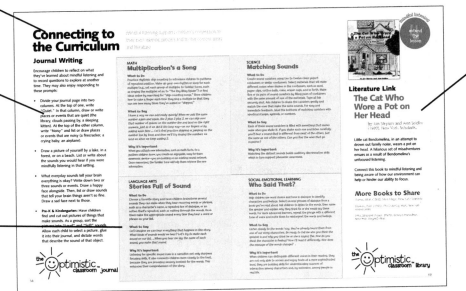

Connecting to the Curriculum

The main lesson is linked to other aspects of children's academic experience: content areas, literature, and writing.

Children are given several prompts for writing and/or drawing in response to the lesson and its target exploration.

Lesson is expanded and extended into three curricular areas and social-emotional learning, connections that can be ongoing as subject-area learning goes on over the course of the school year.

Four literature selections that relate to the lesson focus are recommended for extending the learning.

MindUP Implementation

In order to ensure successful implementation of the MindUP program, consider these points:

- MindUP is not a set of strategies to teach in isolation: the curriculum is meant to be an integral part of a complete classroom life. In deciding when to introduce MindUP lessons, consider how to link MindUP to inquiries you are already engaged in from diverse content areas.

- MindUP lessons depend on both whole-group and small-group discussion. Think about how you can best use the floor space for gathering or arrange desks so that students can see one another.

- MindUP lessons draw on children's life experiences and invite children to look closely at their behaviors—for example, their interactions with peers and family. Bear in mind that some children may prefer not to share, for whatever reasons; give children the option to consider their responses privately, or record them in their journals. Additionally, recalling personal experiences, especially for children with challenging lives outside of school, may bring up unsettling emotions. Creating the Optimistic Classroom, featured in each lesson, has classroom management suggestions that address this and other possibly sensitive situations.

Recommended Implementation Scenarios

MindUP pilot-site teachers have discovered several effective routes to establishing MindUP teaching and practices in their classrooms across the school day and school year. Some of these scenarios are summarized here, followed by an implementation chart to be used for quick reference as you adjust the program to the specific demands of your educational setting, day, and year.

Starting with the Core Practice: At all grade levels, the Core Practice is ideally done three times a day (for a few minutes each time), at intervals suggested below but always adjustable to your needs. (See Lesson 3 for a description of the Core Practice.)

- **Pre-K–2:** Use the Core Practice at start of day (during Circle Time), after recess or lunch, and to "regroup" in preparation for dismissal. The Core Practice, which effectively reins in scattered energy, can also serve as an antidote to end-of-day disruptiveness.

- **Grades 3–5:** Use the Core Practice to begin each day, as an introduction to any daily sharing routine or group announcements you may have in place. This simple routine can also be an extremely useful focus and management tool after recess or lunch, in order to redirect attention to academic subjects— especially before splitting into small groups for collaborative projects.

  Because the Core Practice is aimed in part at making the mind more receptive to learning for understanding, it is an ideal tool before embarking on a new area of study or in preparation for tests that are likely to demand that students "keep their cool" while being asked to summon up stored information.

The Core Practice can be built into your routine summing-up of the day especially as a means for reunifying the class prior to dismissal. The Core Practice by its nature precludes conflict; it is especially effective as a self-regulating skill for upper-elementary students, who are about to experience dramatic physical and emotional changes they may not be well prepared to deal with.

- **Grades 6–8:** By middle school, students are capable of engaging in the Core Practice. As a homeroom, advisory, or content-area instructor, you may wish to build the Core Practice into your class meeting to establish important stability in preparation for the "gear shifting" required as students move among multiple subjects, rooms, and teachers.

  Because the Core Practice prepares the ground for learning, make a point to remind students that they can use it for their own self-regulation and focus when they feel it necessary. This sense of agency is critical for students at this age, as they learn to take responsibility for their own learning and social interactions. In addition, when implementing MindUP at the middle grades, it is extremely helpful to coordinate with other teachers a grade-wide or school-wide plan for incorporating MindUP Core Practice into classroom routines in various contexts across the curriculum and throughout the year.

- **Alternative and Pullout Settings:** Core Practice is a natural to begin and end sessions in after-school, English-language learning, or special needs settings. It brings calm, unity, and focus to individuals and groups, and sets the stage for introducing almost any area of study or collaborative activity.

MindUP Lessons

The 15 MindUP lessons can be presented at regular intervals and in diverse forms throughout the typical 32-week school year.

In the first few weeks of the year, as explained earlier, "Breathe first!" can be your motto. This is the time for children to become acquainted with the Core Practice and habituated to the daily experience of mindful listening and focused attention to their own breathing and thought processes. By the end of about three weeks, classroom routines and schedules are in place and children have adjusted to the new academic profile. At this point you can begin to launch the MindUP curriculum in earnest, working through the program in sequence from Unit I.

Implementation Scenarios: The following recommendations are based on the experience of MindUP pilot teachers at all grade levels. "Chunking" the lessons is entirely adaptable to your classroom needs; below is an approximation of how to approach incorporating MindUP into the generally busy days all teachers face.

Review thoroughly the information in Linking to Brain Research on the second page of the lesson. Plan at least one 15-minute chunk of time to familiarize children with this material, which always deals with some aspect of how the brain works; a second 15-minute session may be advisable in order to solidify that learning.

Getting Ready, on pages 3 and 4 of the lesson, can also be treated as a learning chunk to be repeated or extended as necessary in advance of the core lesson, outlined on the following two pages. The MindUP warm-up is an opportunity to refer back to the Brain Research segment, and to reinforce children's Core Practice competencies as they prepare for the lesson.

Leading the Lesson may take place over a few days, depending on your time and energies and those of the class. You may wish to treat Engage and Explore as one chunk, then move on to Reflect and MindUP in the Real World in a separate meeting. Again, if you have the time to rewind a bit and incorporate previous discoveries, children will always gain from the recap and reinforcement.

The final two pages of the lesson are the most open-ended in terms of time chunking. The adaptability of lesson content to other curriculum areas and the extension of the lesson into reading and writing activities are important assets of MindUP. These extensions can be carried out in several chunks, feasibly encompassing parts of several days or weeks, depending on the organization of your academic curriculum.

Unit I In most classrooms, teachers have found that Unit I is best introduced in concentrated doses over the course of two or three weeks, spending time to become familiar with the brain basics. The self-regulatory routine of the Core Practice will serve as a backdrop for children's discoveries about what is going on inside as they learn and interact. Because the material here is concrete "science information," you may wish to set aside longer chunks of time—20 to 30 minutes—for these foundational lessons, in order to be able to discuss and review as needed.

Units II and III These lessons, numbered 4 through 12, can be covered in 15-minute chunks as outlined above, extending over approximately two weeks. You may wish to occasionally use a 30-minute period to go into depth on lesson segments. However, since a fundamental purpose of MindUP is to apply mindful awareness in other areas of the curriculum and parts of the school day, there is a benefit to working MindUP knowledge into other discussions and practices. The final two pages of each lesson, the Journal, Curriculum, and Literature Links invite extension and ongoing application of the lesson explorations into other parts of the children's day and into the content areas.

Unit IV The final three lessons are geared toward reaching beyond the immediate context of a lesson, applying MindUP insights to behaviors and actions in the larger community or the world. For these lessons, the time frame can be more open-ended, with classroom discussions serving as an anchor for independent work and reflection on how children's skills at self-regulation, self-discipline, and self-examination have affected their confidence and competence.

At each grade level, there are key factors to consider when implementing MindUP.

- **Pre-K–2:** At the earliest grades, a predominant focus of the program will be on the development of children's skills at self-regulation. Children are usually eager to become skilled practitioners of the Core Practice at these early grades. Once the Core Practice has been established, children become more receptive to and engaged in learning in all areas, and more successful at integrating the academic and social considerations of school life. Keeping MindUP an adventurous exploration rooted in self-awareness is key to helping children enjoy and apply the exciting knowledge they will acquire.

- **Grades 3–5:** Students' broadening self-awareness during this period dovetails well with MindUP's introduction of brain science to broaden the base of students' core knowledge. Learning about their own thinking and gaining some control over their thought processes are useful not only for taking in new information but also for responding, as on standardized testing, to somewhat stressful demands that they "show what they know."

- **Grades 6–8:** At middle school, students will increasingly be able to use MindUP as a tool to prepare themselves to learn. As they acquire agency over their own learning and determine with greater independence how to direct their energies, use their time, organize their lives, and interact with their peers, students in grades 6–8 can look to MindUP for both knowledge and practical skills over the course of a school day and school year.

Alternative Settings: MindUP can be implemented in after-school programs as well as in pullout programs for special-needs students or English language learners. The focus in these settings can be on learning the Core Practice; by doing this, you can establish a setting that is receptive to learning—for each child as well as for the group as a whole. The Core Practice can become the beginning and end practice each time you meet; you can reinforce the concepts and principles of MindUP by reminding students of the self-regulation tools at their disposal, as well as the mindful attention they can make habitual in every learning situation.

For all children, paying attention to their own thinking processes and behaviors consistently enhances receptivity to learning in other academic and social-emotional areas.

Implementation Charts

Sample MindUP Lesson Chunking for Grades Pre-K–2 and 3–5

Time	Chunk/Content	Lesson page
10–15 min	Linking to Brain Research & Clarify for the Class	2
10–15 min	Getting Ready, MindUP Warm-Up & Discuss	3–4
10–15 min	Leading the Lesson: Engage & Explore	5
10–15 min	Leading the Lesson: Reflect & MindUP in the Real World	6
(variable)	Extend: Journal Writing*	7
10–15 min	Extend: Connecting to Curriculum*	7–8
10–15 min	Extend: Connecting to Curriculum*	7–8
(variable)	Extend: Literature Link (Independent Reading)*	8

* It is highly recommended that you take advantage of extension links, in order to apply MindUP principles to support and facilitate all kinds of learning.

Sample MindUP Lesson Chunking for Grades 6–8

Time	Chunk/Content	Lesson page
10–15 min	Linking to Brain Research & Clarify for the Class	2
10–15 min	Getting Ready, MindUP Warm-Up & Discuss	3–4
10–15 min	Leading the Lesson: Engage & Explore	5
10–15 min	Leading the Lesson: Reflect & MindUP in the Real World	6
(variable)	Extend: Journal Writing*	7
10–15 min	Extend: Connecting to Curriculum*	7–8
10–15 min	Extend: Connecting to Curriculum*	7–8
(variable)	Extend: Literature Link (Independent Reading)*	8

* It is highly recommended that you take advantage of extension links, in order to apply MindUP principles to support and facilitate all kinds of learning. (Curriculum links may be handled by content area instructors.)

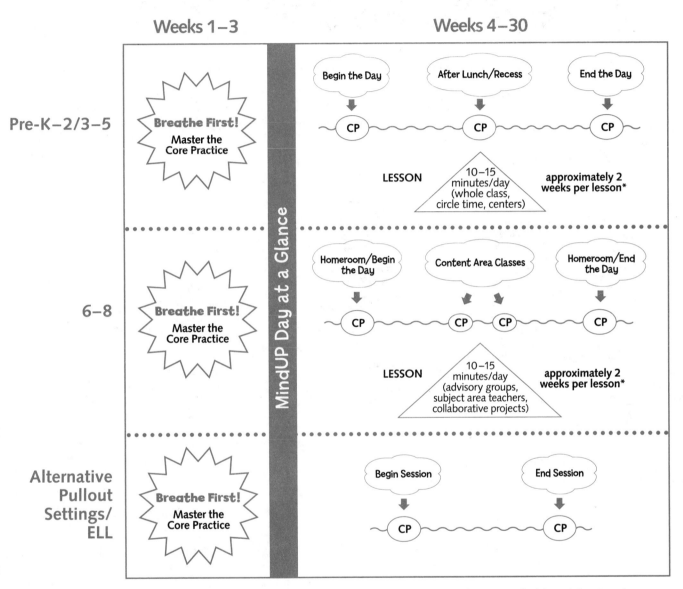

Weeks 1–3   Weeks 4–30

Pre-K–2/3–5

Breathe First! Master the Core Practice

Begin the Day → CP — After Lunch/Recess → CP — End the Day → CP

LESSON — 10–15 minutes/day (whole class, circle time, centers) — approximately 2 weeks per lesson*

6–8

Breathe First! Master the Core Practice

Homeroom/Begin the Day → CP — Content Area Classes → CP CP — Homeroom/End the Day → CP

LESSON — 10–15 minutes/day (advisory groups, subject area teachers, collaborative projects) — approximately 2 weeks per lesson*

Alternative Pullout Settings/ ELL

Breathe First! Master the Core Practice

Begin Session → CP — End Session → CP

MindUP Day at a Glance

* NOTE: Lessons 14 and 15 require student time spent outside of the classroom; schedule and duration of these lessons should be adjusted accordingly.

CP=Core Practice

Getting
Focused

By learning how their brains respond to stress and by practicing strategies for quieting their minds, children become better at self-regulating, increase their capacity for absorbing information, and improve their relationship skills.

Lesson 1:
How Our Brains Work...26

Children learn about the three parts of their brains that help them think and respond to stress.

Lesson 2:
Mindful Awareness....... 34

Children compare two types of behavior: mindful (reflective and purposeful) and unmindful (reflexive and unaware)—and identify the parts of the brain responsible for controlling each type.

Lesson 3:
Focused Awareness: The Core Practice.......... 42

This lesson introduces daily strategies for calming down and paying attention. Children begin to learn ways to help their brains work more mindfully.

Do you ever wonder why high-pressure situations make us "lose our cool"? An accelerated heartbeat and butterflies in the stomach seem to happen no matter how well prepared we are.

The human brain is wired to respond to stress as if something were immediately threatening, often placing us at the mercy of our physical and emotional responses. Yet, we can actually train our brains to respond reflectively. This realization is empowering for students, who deal with many stresses in and out of the classroom—from bullying to homework.

The focus of this unit is on the interplay of three key parts of the brain—the amygdala (reactive center), the prefrontal cortex (reflective center), and the hippocampus (memory and information processing and storage center). Children will learn practical strategies, including listening and breathing exercises, to prime their brains for learning and behaving mindfully.

How Our Brains **Work**

What's So Important About the Brain?

Our brain can serve as a map for showing us how we learn and why we behave the way we do. Neuroscience provides a wealth of information that can help us and our children become better thinkers and healthier people.

Why Introduce Children to Brain Research?

Children are fascinated by facts about their brains. Sharing scientific information about how the brain processes information and is wired to react under stress is a great way to introduce a challenge to your children: How can we learn to react differently, helping our brain make wise choices about our words and actions?

As children become more familiar with three key parts of the brain involved in thinking and learning, they'll begin to understand how their feelings arise—and that they have the ability to change what they do in response. This understanding lays the groundwork for them to monitor and regulate their behavior by calming themselves in the face of anxiety, focusing their attention, and taking control of their learning.

What Can You Expect to Observe?

"Modeling their brain with their two fists not only gives children a sense of the size of the brain, but the activity also makes them more curious. They begin thinking about their brain and asking all sorts of questions. Using nicknames for parts of the brain allows us to talk about them in a meaningful way."

—Pre-K teacher

Linking to Brain Research

Meet Some Key Players in the Brain

The limbic system controls emotions and motivations from deep inside the brain. A key player of the limbic system is the amygdala. The amygdala is a pair of almond-shaped structures that reacts to fear, danger, and threat. The amygdala regulates our emotional state by acting as the brain's "security guard," protecting us from threats. When a child is in a positive emotional state, the amygdala sends incoming information on to the conscious, thinking, reasoning brain. When a child is in a negative emotional state (stressed or fearful, for example) the amygdala prevents the input from passing along, effectively blocking higher-level thinking and reasoned judgment. The incoming stimuli and signals are left for the amygdala itself to process as an automatic reflexive response of "fight, flight, or freeze."

The hippocampus is another limbic system structure. These twin crescent-shaped bodies reside in the central brain area, one behind each ear, in the temporal lobes. The hippocampus assists in managing our response to fear and threats, and is a storage vault of memory and learning.

Information from the limbic system is fed to the prefrontal cortex—the learning, reasoning, and thinking center of the brain. This highly evolved area of the brain controls our decision making, focuses our attention, and allows us to learn to read, write, compute, analyze, predict, comprehend, and interpret.

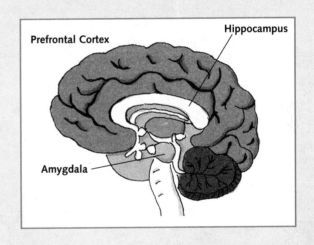

Learning about these key players helps children understand how their brains respond to stress and prepares them for creating a calm mind-set for thoughtful decision making, led by the prefrontal cortex (PFC).

Clarify for the Class

Make a model to show how the brain processes information under stress. Fill a clear plastic bottle with water, an inch of sand, some glitter, and metallic mini-confetti. To demonstrate the way the amygdala on alert scatters information, shake the bottle and mix up the solution. The settling solution represents the calming mind—eventually the bits of information flow in a clear direction, some of them to the PFC for thoughtful decision making.

Discuss: Can you think of a time when your brain feels all shaken up and confused—like the sand, glitter, and confetti in this shaken bottle? What helps you calm down so you can think?

Getting Ready

Picture Your Brain
Using an anatomical drawing and hand gestures, a teacher introduces the parts of the brain.

GOALS
- Children identify the amygdala, the hippocampus, and the prefrontal cortex (PFC) on a diagram of the brain.
- Children will give a simple definition of these three parts of the brain.

MATERIALS
- chart paper and marker
- "Getting to Know and Love Your Brain" poster
- Brain Power! activity sheet (p. 152)

CREATING THE OPTIMISTIC CLASSROOM
Classroom Management In Lesson 2, children will learn the importance of being mindful. Lay the groundwork for children to behave in a mindful way by establishing a set of classroom rules, such as the following:
- Respect others. Treat them as you want to be treated.
- Be kind.
- Listen when someone is speaking.
- Take turns speaking.
- Ask questions when you're curious or confused.
- Stay focused on your own work when the teacher is working with others.
- Celebrate everyone's accomplishments.

Here It Is!
A child shows his partner the location of his prefrontal cortex.

MINDUP Warm-Up

Celebrating the Brain

Expand children's thinking about their brains with the following song:

My Brain Is So Very Important to Me

My brain is so very important; it helps me do most everything,
Located here in my head; it's why I can think, choose, and sing.
My brain, my brain; it is so important to me, to me,
My brain, my brain; it is so important to me.
My brain, it helps me think and remember; my brain tells me fight, flee, or freeze;
It helps all my parts work together, and that's why I just have to say,
My brain, my brain; it is so important to me, to me,
My brain, my brain; it is so important to me.

Write the lyrics on chart paper. Before introducing the song to children, practice singing it several times to the tune of "My Bonnie Lies Over the Ocean." Use gestures and movement to act out the words and phrases.

Discuss: After singing the song with children a few times, ask them to talk about what their brains help them do every day and why they think their brains are so important to them.

Leading the Lesson

Your Brain Is Showing!

Engage

What to Do

Review with children your warm-up activity discussion on the importance of their brains. Then tell them that exercise can help make their brains become stronger.

- We need exercise to make our bodies strong. Running and playing help us make our bodies strong. We need exercise to make our brains strong, too. Thinking helps us make our brains strong.

Explain that together the class will learn about some of the parts of the brain and what each part does. Give each child a copy of the Brain Power! activity sheet and display the "Getting to Know and Love Your Brain" poster for reference. Introduce the three key parts of the brain involved in thinking and acting: the prefrontal cortex, the amygdala, and the hippocampus.

Have children pronounce the terms with you and identify the location of each part. Ask them to point to their own head as a model (PFC: right behind the forehead; amygdala: deep inside, behind each ear; hippocampus: just behind the amygdala on both sides).

Why It's Important

Familiarity with brain parts and their functions helps children begin to think about thinking—how they learn, remember, solve problems, understand themselves and other people. This lays the groundwork for an involvement in their own learning and social interactions.

Explore

What to Do

Have children model their brains by making a fist with each hand and putting their fists together with right and left knuckles aligned and thumbs side by side, pointing upward.

- Your thumbs are the prefrontal cortex. Think of the prefrontal cortex as the wise leader who helps you make good choices and pay attention.

- The tips of your pointer fingers are buried deep inside. They are the amygdala. Think of the amygdala as the security guard, who warns you of danger, keeps you safe, and helps you express emotions, such as anger and fear.

- The tips of your middle fingers are your hippocampus, the saver of memories. This saver of memories keeps important information and brings it back when we need it.

As you name the parts of the brain, have children wiggle their fingers to show each part. Ask them to describe in their own words what each part does.

PRE-K CORNER: Have children use their fists to model the size of their brain. Emphasize the nicknames—wise leader, security guard, and saver of memories.

Why It's Important

Using visual models and nicknames to establish the names and locations of these three parts of the brain engages children, reinforces concepts in several different ways, and helps build a foundation of background knowledge for future lessons.

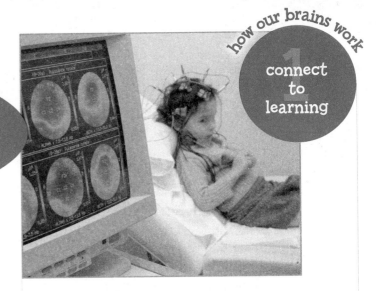

Reflect

To review, have pairs of children retell in their own words the function of each brain part. Guide children to draw a line connecting the name of each part of the brain to its function on the activity sheet. Encourage them to add sketches, notes, and words to help them remember what each part does.

Share a few scenarios to ensure that children can identify the brain parts and their functions.

- Imagine this: You are asleep. A loud crash wakes you up. How does your body immediately react? What are you thinking? How does your body feel?

- Which part of your brain will keep you safe— your brain's wise leader (the prefrontal cortex), your brain's security guard (the amygdala), or your brain's memory saver (the hippocampus)?

Conclude this lesson by sharing with children that future MindUP lessons will help them calm their amygdala when there's no immediate threat, strengthen their ability to focus by getting information to the PFC efficiently, and store important ideas in their hippocampus.

Providing real-life scenarios about different types of reactions and eliciting experiences from children gives them useful examples to attach meaning to. This review lays the groundwork for the next lesson, which connects mindful and unmindful behaviors to the roles of the amygdala and the PFC.

MINDUP
In the Real World

Career Connection

If you're fascinated by the brain and how it works, you might consider a career as a neuroscientist. A neuroscientist is anyone who studies the brain and central nervous system. Within the wide-ranging field of neuroscience, there are many specialized jobs; for example, a *neuroanatomist* studies the structure of the nervous system, while a *neurochemist* investigates how neurotransmitters work. If operating on the brain sounds exciting, consider the work of a *neurosurgeon,* or, if you're concerned about diseases that affect the brain, become a *neuropathologist.* A *neuropsychologist* explores brain-behavior relationships.

Pre-K–2 Discuss: What do you know about the brain? What more would you like to find out? How might you do that?

Once a Day

Take a break to self-assess: do your responses reveal the dominance of your amygdala (reaction) or your PFC (reflection)? If your amygdala is being activated, what is triggering its response? What would you like to change about your style of reaction?

Connecting to the Curriculum

Learning about the brain supports children's connection to their own learning process and to the content areas and literature.

Journal Writing

Encourage children to reflect on what they've learned and to record questions to explore at another time. The youngest children can keep a visual journal for their drawings and early writing efforts. Children may also enjoy responding to these prompts:

- Draw a picture of your brain. Highlight the prefrontal cortex, amygdala, and hippocampus with different colors. Then imagine a scary situation. Draw a speech balloon to each part of your brain. Write how each part reacts.

- Write about or draw a favorite memory that's stored in your hippocampus. Why do you think your prefrontal cortex saved that memory?

- Write a poem about the amygdala, the hippocampus, and the prefrontal cortex. To get started, think about these questions: Why is each part important? How do the parts work together? When does each part go into action?

- Imagine the amygdala, hippocampus, and prefrontal cortex as superheroes. Give each a name to explain its role.

- **Pre-K & Kindergarten:** Ask children to draw a picture of a time when they felt afraid. Record each child's explanation of what happened in his or her journal.

the Optimistic classroom™ journal

MATH
A Calming Countdown

What to Do
Counting to ten can help children deal with stressful situations. Review the numbers from 1 to 10. Then describe an unsettling event such as a sudden, severe thunderstorm. Ask children to respond immediately to it. Have them imagine the same situation. Tell them to count to ten before responding. Discuss the differences in their responses. Point out that the first time, they reacted immediately to the situation; the second time, they had the time to reflect on the situation before responding.

What to Say
Imagine this: You want to play with a favorite toy. A younger child takes it away from you without asking. Quick: What do you do? The next day, the same thing happens. You're playing with your favorite toy, and the same child takes it. Count to ten. What do you do?

Why It's Important
Counting to ten allows children to reflect rather than react to a situation that causes stress. This self-imposed time-out allows the amygdala to pass signals to the PFC. The "wise leader" will make the decision, and in the future, the hippocampus will be able to pull up a positive memory of how to successfully deal with stress, frustration, or upset.

SCIENCE
That's Scary! No, It's Not!

What to Do
Have children draw a simple happy face and unhappy face on separate sheets of paper. Pose different potentially scary or anxiety-producing situations: riding on a roller coaster, seeing a snake, participating in a dance or music recital or a sporting event, and so on. Ask children to hold up a happy face or unhappy face to show how they would respond to each situation.

What to Say
Let's imagine ourselves in a few different situations. How does each situation make us feel? Here's the first one: You're riding on a roller coaster. How does that make you feel? Hold up a happy face or an unhappy face. I'm going to hold up an unhappy face. I see that some of you are NOT scared of riding on a roller coaster!

Why It's Important
Although our brains have the same basic structure, we each respond to situations in unique ways. How our brains operate—how the parts interact in a certain situation—will differ.

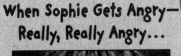
LANGUAGE ARTS
What's My Role?

What to Do
Display the back of the "Getting to Know and Love Your Brain" poster where all can see it. Group children in teams of three or four. Read each question. Have each team agree on an answer. Older children can write down their answers, while younger children can give answers orally. Ask each team to reveal its answer. Post correct answers around the perimeter of the poster. Use yarn or sticky tack to connect questions and answers.

What to Say
I'll ask a question about the parts of the brain we've learned about: the amygdala, hippocampus, and prefrontal cortex. Each team will work together to answer it.
* *This part helps us remember friends' names. [hippocampus]*
* *This part is right behind our forehead. It helps us make good decisions. [prefrontal cortex]*
* *You jump away from a sudden noise. Which part of your brain is at work? [amygdala]*

Why It's Important
As children learn more about their brains, they will find out ways to exercise the parts of their brains, especially the prefrontal cortex, which will help them make good choices, pay attention, and learn more.

SOCIAL-EMOTIONAL LEARNING
Take a Big Breath

What to Do
The more strategies a child has for calming the amygdala, the better. Deep breathing will teach children to focus their attention and relax. Have them stand more than one arm's-length apart, with feet at hip-width. Model the activity first. Repeat at least ten times.

What to Say
Taking big breaths can help calm us down and focus.
* *Stand with your feet apart. Cross one wrist over the other.*
* *Slowly breathe in through your nose. Lift your arms so they meet over your head.*
* *Let out your breath slowly. Bring your arms down and cross your wrists again.*

Why It's Important
Children need to know that they can control their responses with simple techniques, such as deep breathing. Focusing their breathing helps children become calmer.

Literature Link
When Sophie Gets Angry— Really, Really Angry

by Molly Bang
(1999). New York: Scholastic.

In an angry fit, Sophie runs out of her house. As Sophie begins to notice the natural world around her, she calms down and returns home in a better mood.

After reading aloud the book, connect it to how reflecting rather than reacting can have a positive effect on our behavior.

More Books to Share

Cave, Kathryn. (2003). *You've Got Dragons*. Atlanta: Peachtree Publishers.

Kachenmeister, Cherryl. (1989). *On Monday When It Rained*. Boston: Little, Brown, and Company.

Vail, Rachel. (2002). *Sometimes I'm Bombaloo*. New York: Scholastic.

Mindful
Awareness

What Is Mindful Awareness?

Attending to the here and now—other people, the environment, a concern or challenge—in a considerate, nonjudgmental way is called mindful awareness. It's a skill that can be developed by paying close attention to our present situation and our role in it. By reflecting on our thoughts and actions, we can decide how to make better choices when appropriate.

Why Introduce Children to Mindful Awareness?

Learning to be mindfully in tune with what's happening in the moment prepares children to make sound decisions rather than be ruled by their emotions. In Lesson 1, children learned that their brains can produce a well-thought-out reaction by way of the reflective prefrontal cortex or trigger a thoughtless one through the reflexive amygdala. In this lesson, children further explore those contrasting styles of response, using the terms *mindful* and *unmindful* to sort out important thoughts and actions in their own lives. They also discuss the benefits of mindful awareness and learn a focusing strategy for being more mindful.

This lesson provides the language of self-awareness, self-control, and compassionate action that undergirds the rest of the MindUP curriculum.

What Can You Expect to Observe?

"Honestly, I'm working as hard at being mindful as my children are. I share stories of when I have been unmindful and how I try to become more mindful, so my children will see it as a process that we all go through, no matter our age."

—Second-grade teacher

Linking to Brain Research

The Amygdala and Mindful Awareness

The amygdala determines emotional responses by classifying incoming sights, sounds, smells, and movements as either potentially threatening or pleasurable. Input deemed pleasurable goes on to the prefrontal cortex where it is analyzed before it is responded to. Input perceived as threatening is blocked by the amygdala and instead prompts an immediate reflexive reaction—fight, flight, or freeze.

The amygdala does not make a distinction between perceived threats and actual dangers. It can trigger "false alarm" reactive behavior that is unwarranted and potentially problematic. For instance, we sometimes freeze in stressful situations, such as taking a test. This is an example of unmindful behavior. A reaction happens before the mind thinks about it. Conversely, when we consciously process sensory input, we create a time buffer between the input and the response. This gives the prefrontal cortex time to analyze, interpret, and prioritize information, allowing us to choose the best course of action. We call this mindful behavior. A response happens *after* our mind thinks about it.

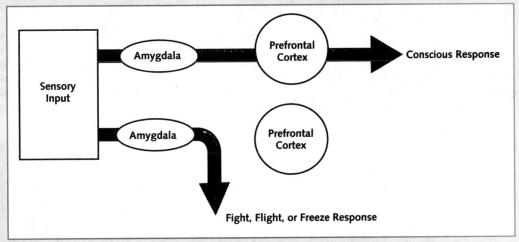

Unmindful thoughts and actions occur when the gate-keeper amygdala blocks the flow of sensory input to the prefrontal cortex and unconsciously reacts.

Clarify for the Class

Explain that thinking mindfully happens when our brain has time to think about what we hear or see before we respond to it. An example is "counting to ten" when we're frustrated or angry. By the time we get to ten, we feel better and can think more clearly—and mindfully.

Discuss: Have any of you ever counted to ten when you've gotten angry? Did it help? How? What do you think happened in your brain during the time it took to count?

Getting Ready

Mindful Us!
Children practice speaking and listening mindfully to a partner.

GOALS

- Children define and describe the difference between mindful and unmindful thoughts and actions.
- Children apply the concept of mindful awareness to their own lives.

MATERIALS

- chart paper
- Mindful or Unmindful? activity sheet (p. 153)

CREATING THE OPTIMISTIC CLASSROOM

ELL Classroom Management During the day, take the time to celebrate moments of your children's mindful behavior. Create a running chart of these celebrations, which might include statements such as the following:

- Carlos thought before he acted.
- Kenisha focused when she listened to the story.
- Leo took deep breaths to help him focus on the math problem.

To help ELL children recognize mindful behaviors, use an icon on the chart, such as a glowing light bulb. Try to snap photos of the children in action and include them on the chart.

**Catching Every
Sound**
Children listen with full
attention to the sounds
around them.

MINDUP Warm-Up

Focusing on Sounds Practice

Give children a context for understanding mindful awareness through an auditory focusing exercise.

Review the five senses with children. Then tell them that they are going to focus on using their ears to hear the sounds around them.

Ask children to sit comfortably and close or cover their eyes and then listen very carefully for all the sounds they can hear around them in the classroom, the hallway, and elsewhere inside and outside the school. After 30 seconds, tell children to open their eyes and share the sounds they heard. First, have them turn and talk to a partner to compare the sounds they heard. Then record on chart paper the sounds they heard. This can also be done as a shared writing practice.

Repeat the activity. Encourage children to listen for sounds they didn't hear the first time and have them share the results.

PRE-K CORNER: Limit the listening time for younger children to 15–20 seconds or less. Their listening stamina will build as they continue to do these auditory exercises.

Discuss: How did sitting and listening make you feel? Were you surprised by all the different sounds you heard around you? Those sounds are always there. We don't hear them when we're busy working in the classroom. We are not directing our brain to listen for the sounds.

Leading the Lesson

Learning to Be Mindful

Engage	Explore

What to Do

Talk about the warm-up exercise. Connect it to what children have learned about the parts of the brain.

- Wasn't it surprising how many sounds we heard when we just sat and listened? The parts of our brain worked together to help us pay attention to the sounds around us. Our amygdala, our security guard, let lots of sound information through to our PFC, our wise leader. Then the PFC sent the information to our memory saver, the hippocampus.

Explain to children that when they were listening, they were being mindful.

- When you listened so well, you were being mindful. You were paying attention as well as you could to the sounds around you. When we are being mindful, we think before we act.

- When we're being unmindful, we act without thinking. We aren't paying attention to what's happening around us. The amygdala, our security guard, tries to do all the work for our brain.

Help children see the difference between mindful behavior and its opposite, unmindful behavior. Share an example to contrast the two behaviors.

- Here is an example of being mindful: You taste a food to decide whether you like it.

- Here is an example of being unmindful: You see a food and immediately decide you don't like it. You declare that you don't like orange food.

- In fact, not all orange food tastes the same. If you taste something, you might find out that you really do like it.

Read aloud each example from the Mindful or Unmindful? activity sheet and have children put their thumb up if the behavior described seems mindful or down if the behavior seems unmindful. Give children a chance to explain their reasoning.

- Listen as I read each example. Which one shows mindful behavior? Which one shows unmindful behavior?

Why It's Important

Mindful awareness can be described as "focusing without judgment." It is experiencing the here and now without making snap judgments. By noticing what they're thinking and feeling, children can allow their thoughts and feelings to come and go. They are choosing to be mindful.

Having children evaluate decisions that they can relate to, such as the ones described on the activity sheet (e.g., helping someone with special needs or trying a new food for the first time), helps them begin to make connections with their own thoughts and behaviors. Be careful, however, that children do not equate "mindful" with "good" behavior or "unmindful" with "bad" behavior.

Reflect

Ask children to share stories about times when they were mindful. You might kick off the discussion by sharing your own anecdote.

Reassure children that all of us are occasionally unmindful, and that through practice—really thinking about what we're about to say or do—we can more often make mindful choices that will help ourselves and the people around us.

- Being mindful takes practice. We're going to do our best to be mindful. We are going to try to think before we speak or act. We're going to let the parts of our brain work together.

- When we see unmindful behavior, we can nicely remind one another and ourselves to "use your PFC, please!"

Conclude this lesson by celebrating children's stories of being mindful. Write children's statements and post them to remind the class of examples of mindful behaviors (see Creating the Optimistic Classroom box, page 36).

Encouraging children to evaluate memorable actions in their lives as mindful or unmindful behavior gives them useful examples to attach meaning to. Being unmindful does not mean that we are bad people— but it probably means that our amygdala is more in charge than our PFC. Reflecting on unmindful decisions simply gives us an opportunity to make ourselves and the people around us safer, healthier, and happier.

MINDUP
In the Real World

Career Connection

An emergency medical technician (EMT), often the first to arrive at the scene of an accident, is trained to remain calm and focus on what has happened and what immediate action is required. EMTs are typically dispatched to an emergency scene by a 911 operator and often work with police or fire departments. All EMTs must know how to assess an emergency, control bleeding, apply splints, assist with childbirth, administer oxygen, and perform CPR and other basic life support skills. Mindfulness that enables quick, decisive thinking is the EMT's most essential skill.

Discuss: What are you really good at paying attention to? What jobs do people do around this school that you think really demand mindful attention and why?

Once a Day

Share with children an observation about a mindful decision you or a student made in a demanding situation. Reflect on how your PFC may have guided your choice.

Connecting to the Curriculum

Learning about mindful behavior supports children's connection to their own learning process and to the content areas and literature.

Journal Writing

Encourage children to reflect on what they've learned about being mindful and to record questions to explore at another time. Children may also enjoy responding to these prompts:

- Choose one of these scenes of unmindful behavior. Write and/or draw a picture about what might happen next.
  1. A child is looking up at the sky and is about to walk into a tree.
  2. A child is playing baseball. His or her shoes are tied in a sloppy way.
  3. A child leaves the door open. A dog looks out the open door at a squirrel.

- Write the words "MINDFUL ME" on one page of your journal and the words "UNMINDFUL ME" on the next page. Draw a picture of yourself to go with each. Use speech bubbles to show the words you might be saying.

- Tell your family about our listening activity. Ask them to sit with you and listen to the sounds around them. Record what you hear in words and/or pictures.

- **Pre-K & Kindergarten:** Ask children to draw a picture of themselves doing an activity they enjoy. Label the activity and write "Mindful Me" on each picture.

LANGUAGE ARTS
A Mind Full of Words

What to Do
Throughout the MindUP lessons, children will repeatedly hear terms introduced in this lesson, including *mindful, unmindful, focus,* and *attention.* Use a variety of methods—demonstration, acting out, drawing—to reinforce the meanings of these words. For example, you might use the focusing function on a projector to show an image both in and out of focus.

What to Say
See how the picture changes? When the picture is in focus, it becomes clear. The same thing happens when we focus our attention. When we really focus on a math problem, it becomes clear. Now you know what it means to be focused. Can you think of a way to draw a picture for the word focus so you will remember it?

Why It's Important
To get the full benefit of MindUp lessons, children will need to know a specific vocabulary. Participating in peer discussions will help reinforce children's understanding of the words and their meanings.

SOCIAL STUDIES
Keep Me in Mind

What to Do
Draw a word web on chart paper or the board. Write "A Mindful Person" at the top. Ask children to think of people at school who act in mindful ways, such as the custodian. Write the name in the center circle of the word web. Brainstorm a list of mindful behaviors that the person exhibits and write them on the word web.

What to Say
Many people work in our school, both outside and inside. They must work in mindful ways. Choose one person. What is his or her job? How does this person act in a mindful way? What kind of important decisions does this person make?

Why It's Important
Having a role model at school reinforces children's understanding of what it means to behave in a mindful way. They can look to that person as an example and even ask the person questions about how they think before making decisions. This activity also encourages children to focus on the world around them.

SCIENCE
Taking Care of Our Environment

What to Do
One morning before class starts, toss pieces of crumpled paper around the trash can or recycling container. If children don't initiate a discussion about the trash, start one yourself. Begin by catching yourself in the act of being unmindful and tossing another piece of paper on the ground. Ask children why it's important to be mindful of our environment and to keep it clean and free of trash.

What to Say
Oops! Look what I've done! What a mess! I wasn't paying any attention to what I was doing. Would you help me put the paper in the trash can? Thank you. Why is it important for all of us to be mindful of our environment? What would happen to our environment if we acted in an unmindful way? What are some things we can do to take care of our environment?

Why It's Important
Children make the connection between their actions and the world around them. Being mindful is a continual practice that extends beyond the walls of their classroom.

SOCIAL-EMOTIONAL LEARNING
Let's Play in a Mindful Way

What to Do
Ask pairs or small groups of children to create posters that show some of the school's playground rules. You may want to write some of these rules on chart paper or the board if they are not already on display. Have each pair or group choose one rule to illustrate. Urge children to think about the reasons for the rule. Why is the rule important? How does it promote behaving in a mindful way?

What to Say
We have a set of rules for how to behave on the playground. Why is it important to have these rules? How do rules help us behave in a more mindful way? Look at this list of rules. Choose one rule to depict. Write a sentence about why this rule is important. How does it help change unmindful behavior to mindful behavior?

Why It's Important
When children represent and share mindful actions that should occur on the playground, they internalize ways in which they are already acting mindfully. This promotes their awareness of the larger community.

Literature Link
How Do Dinosaurs Eat Their Food?
by Jane Yolen
(2005). New York: Scholastic.

When dinosaurs eat their food, some are mindful—and mind their manners. Lambeosaurus, for example, takes a bite of everything. Clearly, the prefrontal cortex is wisely guiding this dinosaur's choices about what to eat. On the other hand, Spinosaurus chews and then spits out the broccoli.

As you read aloud this book, stop periodically to allow children to identify the dinosaurs' behavior as mindful or unmindful. Ask them which part of the brain is in charge in each case.

More Books to Share
Bryan, Sean. (2007). *A Bear and His Boy*. New York: Arcade Publishing.

Moroney, Lynn. (1989). *Baby Rattlesnake*. San Francisco: Children's Book Press.

Williams, Mary. (1996). *Cool Cats, Calm Kids*. San Luis Obispo, CA: Impact Publishers.

the **Optimistic** classroom™ library

Focused Awareness:
The Core Practice

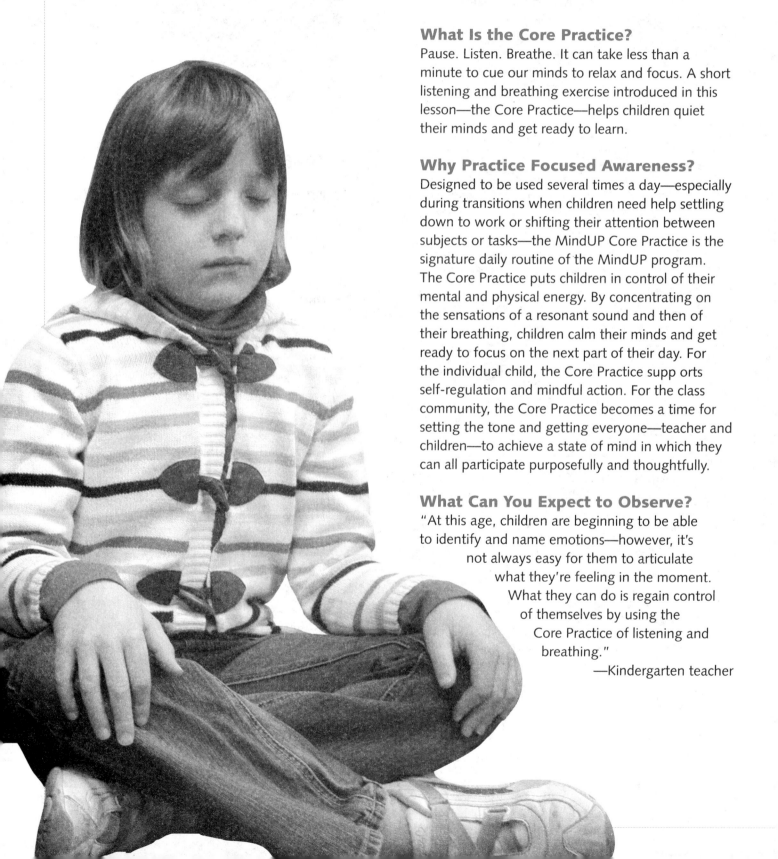

What Is the Core Practice?

Pause. Listen. Breathe. It can take less than a minute to cue our minds to relax and focus. A short listening and breathing exercise introduced in this lesson—the Core Practice—helps children quiet their minds and get ready to learn.

Why Practice Focused Awareness?

Designed to be used several times a day—especially during transitions when children need help settling down to work or shifting their attention between subjects or tasks—the MindUP Core Practice is the signature daily routine of the MindUP program. The Core Practice puts children in control of their mental and physical energy. By concentrating on the sensations of a resonant sound and then of their breathing, children calm their minds and get ready to focus on the next part of their day. For the individual child, the Core Practice supp orts self-regulation and mindful action. For the class community, the Core Practice becomes a time for setting the tone and getting everyone—teacher and children—to achieve a state of mind in which they can all participate purposefully and thoughtfully.

What Can You Expect to Observe?

"At this age, children are beginning to be able to identify and name emotions—however, it's not always easy for them to articulate what they're feeling in the moment. What they can do is regain control of themselves by using the Core Practice of listening and breathing."
—Kindergarten teacher

Linking to Brain Research

Controlling Our Breathing

Focusing on breathing helps calm the body by slowing heart rate, lowering blood pressure, and sharpening focus. Paying attention to breathing also supports strong functioning in the higher brain. Controlled breathing lessens anxiety by overriding the "fight, flight, or freeze" response set off by the amygdala and gives control to conscious thought, which takes place in the prefrontal cortex. When breathing is deliberately regulated, the brain is primed to think first and then plan a response, enabling mindful behavior.

Teaching children to focus on and control their breathing can help them become less reactive and more reflective when feeling anxious or stressed. The short daily activity of listening and breathing (Core Practice) introduced in this lesson capitalizes on neuroplasticity, the brain process that creates and strengthens nerve cell (neuron) connections through practice or repeated experience. One example of this growth occurs on the receiving end of the neurons involved in repeated thoughts and actions; branch-like receptors called dendrites increase in number and size, enabling a more efficient passage of information along frequently used neural pathways. This is one of many ways in which the structure of the brain is flexible and ready to grow.

As children practice controlled breathing, their brains develop and reinforce the "habit" of responding to anxiety by focusing on breathing. This leads to reflective rather than reactive responses. The more controlled breathing is practiced, the more self-managed and mindful children can become.

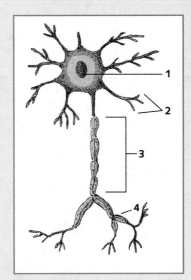

Nerve cells, or neurons, carry messages through electrochemical impulses or signals. The cell body (soma) [1] houses the neuron's control center (nucleus). Dendrites [2] receive information from other neurons. The axon [3] relays the signal from the dendrites to [4] the nerve endings, which transmit the information to other neurons.

Clarify for the Class

Have children use their hand and forearm to show the parts of a neuron: The palm is the nucleus, the fingers are dendrites, the forearm is the axon, and the elbow (with two or three sticky flags attached) is the nerve ending. Show how the information moves from the dendrites through the axon and gets sent along to another neuron's dendrites (children can link up fingers to elbows to create an information path).

Discuss: Can you show in your model which part of our brain cells grow when we practice something? What do you think will happen to the neurons in charge of helping us focus when we practice mindful breathing?

Getting Ready

Resonant Sound!
Striking a gentle but resonant instrument creates the opening and closing note of the Core Practice.

GOALS
- Children learn an exercise that combines listening and breathing to calm and focus their minds.
- Children discover the importance of practicing focusing exercises regularly.

MATERIALS
- chart paper
- instrument that resonates with a clear, distinctive tone for 10–20 seconds (e.g., triangle, xylophone, chimes, piano, bell, a violin)

CREATING THE OPTIMISTIC CLASSROOM
Classroom Management As children regularly exercise control of their breathing, a new "brain habit"—one that automatically reacts to anxiety by taking control of breathing—becomes the default pathway leading to reflective rather than reactive responses. The more controlled breathing is practiced, the more self-managed and mindful children can become. The one-minute Core Practice is done three times daily, establishing scheduled opportunities for children to focus and regulate themselves throughout the day.

Deep Belly Breath
A child feels her lungs expand
and contract as she breathes
deeply.

MINDUP Warm-Up

Focusing on Breathing Practice

Remind children of the mindful exercise they practiced in Lesson 2 when they listened for all the sounds around them. Explain that now they'll be doing another exercise. They'll learn to breathe in a way that helps their brain think more clearly. Modify the following script to guide children through a simple breathing exercise:

• *Sit down in a comfortable position. Close your eyes or look down at your hands.*
• *Pay attention to your breathing.*
• *Take calm, slow breaths. Gently breathe in through your nose, then let go of each breath.*
• *Keep your shoulders relaxed. Picture the air coming into your body and going out again.*
• *If your mind tries to think about other things, bring your attention back to your breath.*
• *Feel your stomach rising and falling. Keep your belly soft and relaxed.*
• *Open your eyes slowly and take another slow, deep breath with your eyes open.*

Discuss: How did you feel as you breathed in and out? What did you notice about your breathing? How did you keep your mind focused on your breathing?

Leading the Lesson

Introducing the Core Practice

Engage	Explore

What to Do

Show children the instrument you will be using for the Core Practice. Play a note to show how it works. Encourage children to talk about the sound; for example, to describe the sound and identify other objects or actions that have a similar sound. If you have the time, allow each child to strike a note.

- I will use this sound to begin and end the exercise. We'll do this exercise together every day. Let's practice listening to the sound as well as we can for as long as it lasts.

Ask children to prepare themselves by: sitting cross-legged in a circle on the floor; resting their hands naturally in their laps or palms up on their knees; closing their eyes or looking down at their hands.

Before you play the sound, tell children to try to focus only on it until they can no longer hear it; when the sound has faded completely, they may open their eyes. Ask: Was it difficult to keep listening? How did you stay focused on listening? Repeat the exercise. Ask children to be aware of their body. Were your shoulders relaxed? Are your hands still?

Prepare children for combining mindful listening with mindful breathing to begin the Core Practice.

Explain the combined exercise.

- To start our Core Practice, we sit comfortably and close our eyes or look down at our hands.

- When you hear the instrument, listen as long and as carefully as you can.

- When the sound has faded completely, begin to focus on each breath.

- When you hear the sound again, listen as long and as carefully as you can. Keep breathing calmly.

- When you can't hear the sound any longer, slowly open your eyes. Remain still and quiet.

Make sure that children understand the directions. Then play a note from the instrument. Pause for at least ten seconds after the sound has stopped, for mindful breathing. Play the note a second time, and observe as children open their eyes.

Why It's Important

Once children have practiced this exercise with the same resonant sound several times, their brains will begin to connect the sound with paying closer attention and being mindful of the moment This resonant sound will become a signal for beginning and ending the Core Practices, so it is essential that you use the same resonant instrument consistently.

Sitting cross-legged on the floor with the head "floating" above the shoulders encourages good posture, breathing, and circulation, which in turn support an alert mind.

Children who are uncomfortable closing their eyes can simply look down at their hands. The most important thing is to avoid visual distractions, especially eye contact, during the exercise.

From the Research
Neuroimaging studies...have revealed that students' comfort level has critical impact on information transmission and storage in the brain. (Ashby, 1999)

Reflect

Encourage children to share their experiences with the Core Practice. Tie in the parts of the brain.

- What do you think was happening in your brain during the Core Practice exercise? What do you think each part of your brain was doing?

Explain that although this exercise may feel awkward at first, their brain will get better at it with practice.

You might point out some challenges you have had during Core Practice, such as keeping your attention focused on your breathing, focusing your listening exclusively on the sound of the instrument, and/or staying still.

Announce the times during the day that children will practice their new listening and breathing skills. Encourage children to try controlled breathing on their own, as well—especially when they are feeling nervous, angry, or afraid.

- We'll do the Core Practice together three times every day. You can do it on your own, too. It will help you stay calm and make good decisions.

When children do the exercise in a mindful, focused way, they establish a precedent that they can follow. Assure children who have trouble staying focused that keeping their concentration on the sound and on their breathing simply takes practice.

Keep a consistent schedule for leading the Core Practice three times a day, ensuring that children are seated and silent before you begin.

MINDUP
In the Real World

Career Connection

Listen, aim, focus, breathe, shoot. We can see that the Core Practice helps us every day no matter what we're doing. One profession that really depends on mindful breathing and listening is that of the wildlife photographer. We owe our most spectacular wildlife photography to the mindful steps the photographer follows before each shot. Sometimes enduring months in remote, challenging environments stalking an elusive animal like the snow leopard, the photographer must listen intently to know when the animal is near and breathe mindfully to assure a steady hand and an in-focus photograph snapped at exactly the right moment.

Discuss: Have you ever done a task for which you had to be very still and center all your attention on what you were doing? What was it? What are some other tasks that might require you to focus like that?

Once a Day

Do one minute of mindful breathing or listen to a piece of calming music just prior to a task or part of your day that demands your full concentration and focus.

Connecting to the Curriculum

Learning about focused awareness supports children's connection to their own learning process and to the content areas and literature.

Journal Writing

Encourage children to reflect on what they've learned about the Core Practice and to record questions to explore at another time. They may also enjoy responding to these prompts:

• Use different colors to show how you feel before, during, and after mindful listening and breathing. Label the colors Before, During, and After.

• Think about practicing mindful listening and breathing at home. Write about or draw the place in your home where you would practice. Also write about or draw the instrument you would use to produce the sound.

• Think about a character in a story who could have used mindful breathing to calm down. Use words and/or pictures to describe how the story might change.

• **Pre-K & Kindergarten:** Let children use finger puppets to show the effect of mindful listening and breathing. Record their observations in their visual journals.

SCIENCE AND ART
The Air in Our Lungs

What to Do
Ask children to place their hands on their chests and feel their lungs fill with air as they breathe in and out. Introduce the words *inhale* and *exhale*. Then, inflate several balloons of different colors. Fill several shallow bowls with paint to match the colors of the balloons. Place a balloon in each bowl. Have children paint pictures by gently bouncing the paint-covered balloons on paper.

What to Say
Can you feel the air going in and out of your lungs as you breathe? When you breathe in, you inhale. When you breathe out, you exhale. When I blow up these balloons, I inhale and then exhale. The air moves from my lungs into the balloons.

I'll place a balloon in each bowl of paint. Gently move the balloon over the sheet of paper to make a painting.

Why It's Important
This activity gives younger children practice with vocabulary and concepts associated with mindful breathing. Watching you inhale and exhale deeply to inflate the balloons reinforces the idea of breathing deeply. Children can see the power of breathing.

PHYSICAL EDUCATION
Breathing Deeply

What to Do
Ask children to lie down on their backs. Place a small object, such as a domino, on their stomachs. Model how you monitor the depth and evenness of your breaths by watching the object rise and fall as you inhale and exhale. Share some of the benefits of deep breathing: It relaxes our bodies; it calms our minds; it makes us able to play a sport longer, and so on.

What to Say
I'm going to see how deeply I can breathe. I'll lie down and put this domino on my belly. Now, I'll breathe in . . . and then out. See how the domino moves up and down with each breath? I'm trying to breathe evenly so the domino moves up and down smoothly. Watching the domino helps me learn how to control my breathing.

Why It's Important
Deep belly breathing gives the lungs even more room to expand than does chest breathing, which tends to produce shallower breaths. This is a good exercise to introduce after a high-energy activity, such as recess.

the Optimistic classroom™ journal

MATH
Graphing Breaths

What to Do
Time children for 15 seconds and count their breaths—one cycle of inhalation and exhalation counts as one. Take three readings: one after intense physical activity, one during a mindful breathing exercise, and one when children are sitting in the classroom. You may also have pairs count and record each other's breaths. Model how to create a bar graph showing the three readings. Compare the readings and discuss the similarities and differences among them.

What to Say
We counted our breaths in three different situations. Then we graphed the results. When did you take the most breaths? When did you take the fewest?

Why It's Important
This activity can help show children when to use mindful breathing to calm themselves. The bar graph also aids in demonstrating how deeply they are breathing during the Core Practice.

Pre-K Corner: Instead of creating a bar graph, focus on counting breaths. Write the numbers on the board or chart paper and invite children to read along as you record the numbers.

SOCIAL-EMOTIONAL LEARNING
Sharing the Practice

What to Do
Once children are familiar and comfortable with the Core Practice, encourage them to do it at home. Talk about the importance of finding a quiet place and a suitable sound maker. Suggest that children guide their families in mindful listening and breathing. Send home a sheet explaining the sequence (see page 46).

What to Say
You all are doing so well with your mindful listening and breathing, why not teach the Core Practice to your family? Think about where you could do the Core Practice at home. Which room could you use? How would you make the sound?

Why It's Important
Teaching their families how to do the Core Practices will give children confidence in their abilities and will allow them to share what they are learning. Every member of the family can benefit from learning how to relax and clear his or her mind.

Literature Link
The Busy Body Book

by Lizzy Rockwell
(2004). New York: Scholastic.

A healthy body and mind are key to focusing awareness. You'll find many ways to dip into this amazing book to share the ways in which the brain, respiration and other body systems work. This book also emphasizes the importance of keeping active, eating well, and getting rest to good health.

More Books to Share

Lite, Lori. (1996). *A Boy and a Bear*. Plantation, FL: Specialty Press.

Ross, Tony. (1983). *Naughty Nicky*. New York: Holt, Rinehart, and Winston.

Showers, Paul, (1992). *The Listening Walk*. New York: HarperCollins.

Sharpening Your Senses

By mindfully observing their senses, students will become adept at sharpening their attention and using sensory experiences to enhance memory, problem solving, relationships, creativity, and physical performance.

Expanding on Lessons 2 and 3, students practice honing their skills in focused listening by participating in an auditory awareness activity.

This lesson demonstrates and emphasizes the importance of paying close attention to detail, using visual memory.

Students use their sense of smell to help focus their attention and gain access to key memories and feelings.

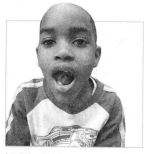

Slowing down to focus on the taste of food can completely change a routine activity and make it a mindful, healthful experience.

Comparing and contrasting excited and calm states of the body helps students make important connections between physical sensations and stress levels.

Students learn two balancing postures that foster awareness of how healthful movement practice can improve physical, emotional, and social well-being.

If you can detect a scent of basil as you walk by a restaurant or spot a contact lens that's dropped on a tile floor, your brain is well trained to zero in on important sensory details.

That same ability to notice important details and differentiate among all the scents, sounds, visual images, and other sensory details your brain receives can also help you respond more mindfully to people and events around you.

We know that each time students deliberately focus their attention, as they do in this unit's lessons, they activate their sensory data filter, the reticular activating system, and its pathways to the prefrontal cortex. This repeated stimulation makes the neural circuits stronger.

The practice of focused, mindful awareness enhances the ability of all young learners to direct their attention where it is needed.

Mindful Listening

What Is Mindful Listening?

From the buzz of a cell phone to the wail of a siren, sounds are all around us. Mindful listening helps us choose which sounds to focus our attention on and helps us to be thoughtful in the way we hear and respond to the words of others.

Why Practice Mindful Listening?

Research suggests that children become more focused and responsive to their environment by participating in mindful listening activities, such as Guess That Sound in this lesson. In fact, training our brains to concentrate on specific sounds helps heighten our sensory awareness. As children monitor their own auditory experience—noting what they choose to focus on and/or respond to—they build self-awareness and self-management skills. Mindful listening also lays the groundwork for social awareness and effective communication—an important part of the Common Core State Standards.

Being able to listen in a focused way to what others say and to home in on important words and phrases give a young listener more context for understanding what's being said and a better idea for how to respond. This work helps prepare children for following directions, resolving conflicts through discussion, building friendships, and listening for important details in texts read aloud.

What Can You Expect to Observe?

"Children love making a game of identifying familiar sounds. They are eager to practice their listening skills because right away they see an improvement in their ability to isolate and identify sounds. This supports our phonemic awareness work: the class is more interested in—and now has more skills in—breaking apart sounds in words."

—Kindergarten teacher

Linking to Brain Research

What Is the RAS?

An intricate network of long nerve pathways lies within the core of the brain stem. This reticular formation, also called the reticular activating system (RAS), helps regulate many basic body functions and connects the brain stem to the prefrontal cortex (PFC) and other parts of the brain. The RAS is a mechanism for keeping the brain awake and alert and is the brain's attention-focusing center. Sensory stimuli (visual, auditory, tactile, olfactory, taste) continually arrive via the spinal cord and are sorted and screened by the RAS. The sensory input deemed relevant by the RAS is routed on to its appropriate destination in the conscious brain. What's irrelevant is blocked.

The RAS is critically important because the brain cannot process the millions of bits of sensory information coming in at once! A child sitting in a classroom likely has competing sensory experiences, such as the voice of her teacher, a wiggly loose tooth, the sight of rain spattering the windowsill, and the aroma of food from the cafeteria. A mindful, focused student is able to redirect her attention to the task at hand, reassuring herself that lunchtime will come after math.

Athletes, musicians, scholars, and other "focused" people have "trained" their RAS to choose the most pertinent sensory stimuli. With practice focusing on specific details, children can train their RAS to be more effective. Such practice is especially important for children who have trouble focusing their attention on their work, instructions, or social cues. Sensory awareness activities in this lesson and the others in this unit provide children with repeated RAS-strengthening practice.

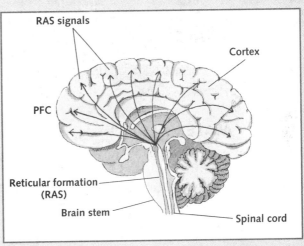

The RAS serves as an "executive personal secretary" to the PFC, forwarding on only what's immediately relevant.

Clarify for the Class

Make a model of the RAS using a kitchen strainer, sugar, and lentils or split peas. Demonstrate how a strainer works. Much like the RAS, it filters input, allowing only some things to pass through. Explain that the RAS lets important sights, sounds, feelings, tastes, and smells pass on to the brain, just as the filter lets sugar pass through. But it blocks unwanted material, just as the strainer blocks the lentils.

Discuss: What are some situations, places, or times of day when it's hard for you to pay attention? When that happens, what do you think is happening in your brain?

Getting Ready

What's that sound?
Children guess what hidden object their teacher is using to make a sound.

GOALS
- Children train their attention on specific sounds and try to identify those sounds.
- Children learn how mindful listening skills can help them communicate more successfully.

MATERIALS
- various common objects for creating sounds
- bag for holding the objects
- Sounds & Scents activity sheet (p. 154)

CREATING THE OPTIMISTIC CLASSROOM

Classroom Management Once a week at circle time, invite pairs of children to use puppets to role-play a simple conversation that targets a communication skill they need practice with (for example, asking a peer to share a book, tool, or toy). Suggest a scenario and have children act it out first in an unmindful, unfriendly way and then in a mindful, friendly way. Ask the class to discuss the differences between the two conversations (e.g., the way words were used and the tone—polite, angry, frustrated, and so on). Guide children to understand that choosing their words carefully with a friendly intention can positively affect how they get along with others.

Aha!
A student guesses correctly
and reveals a retractable
"clicking" pen.

MINDUP Warm-Up

Mindful Listening Practice

Choose a song with parts that are easy to identify, such as vocals, drums, harmonica, cymbals, or violin, and have children gather in a circle on the rug to experience the music. Tell them that you are going to play them a song with special sounds and ask them to listen very carefully to the music so that they can enjoy all the different parts. As they listen to the song the first time, have them put their thumb up each time they hear a new sound or part. Afterward, list on the board the sounds they heard.

Before you play the song a second time, organize children into groups that will each listen for the sound of a specific instrument or part. Invite the groups to stand or do a special movement each time they hear their special sound and sit when they no longer hear the sound. (For younger children, start with two groups and two different sounds or simply focus on a single recurring sound that the whole group listens for.)

Discuss: How did this kind of listening help you enjoy the music? Let's pretend each sound was the voice of someone we know. Whose voices do you listen carefully for at home? in school?

Leading the Lesson

Guess That Sound

Engage | Explore

What to Do

Review mindfulness and the parts of the brain from Unit I, as needed. Initiate a discussion about listening.

○ Let's think about why careful, mindful listening is so important: Can you think of a time when you paid attention with your ears and heard an important sound that warned you about danger?

• What do you do when there's a lot of noise around you to help you pay attention to just one sound, such as a friend's voice on the playground?

Explain that together, the class will participate in a guessing game that will help them practice mindful listening.

Ask children to close their eyes and sit comfortably on the carpet or at their desks. Place in a bag the first object you've gathered that can be used to produce a recognizable sound.

• Listen as mindfully as you can to the sound I make and focus on it until you no longer hear it. If you think you know what it is, keep it a secret and raise your hand.

One at a time, make a sound with each object, then place the object in the bag. Possible sound-producing actions include:
–crumple a piece of paper   –shake coins in a jar
–tap a pencil   –shuffle a deck of cards

Call on several children to share what the sound reminded them of and to make a prediction about what the object and action might have been. For each sound, let a child who's made a prediction pick the object out of the bag and reveal it to the class.

You may want to have older children record their answers on the Sounds & Scents activity sheet. Encourage them to include specific descriptions of each sound and note what each sound made them think about. Reveal the identity of the sound-makers after children have shared their observations.

Why It's Important

There are many sounds surrounding us most of the time. Usually we aren't mindful of every sound, because our brain helps us pay attention: it screens the sounds our ears pick up and brings to our attention only the ones that are important. The sound filter in our brain is called the Reticular Activating System, or RAS. Listening mindfully can help the RAS do a better job.

By paying close attention to specific sounds, you can train your RAS to listen very carefully. That helps the information reach the PFC easily—so you can get the information you're listening for right away.

You are more in control of how you think and how you behave when you pay attention to what you see, hear, taste, touch, and smell.

Reflect

Initiate a class discussion. Make sure children understand that they were using brain energy to identify each sound.

- How is this listening game different from the way we usually listen to sounds?

- If you had trouble concentrating on the sounds, explain what you think distracted you or got in the way.

- How was trying to figure out the different sounds good practice for mindful listening?

Record student responses on chart paper.

When you're really listening well, you get the information you need without being distracted. Then you can mindfully decide what to say or what to do.

MINDUP
In the Real World

Career Connection

Is mindful listening ever a matter of life and death? Sometimes, YES! Every day, doctors practice mindful listening on the job. Not only do they need to listen carefully to their patients' bodies—hearts, lungs, and abdomens—but also to the patients themselves. What brings the patient to the doctor? What symptoms is he or she experiencing? Doctors work hard to learn the skill of active listening. Once the patient's medical history is recorded, the doctor can ask informed questions and order the right tests that will lead to the correct diagnosis and effective treatment. In the hospital, mindful listening saves people's lives.

Discuss with children how this and other careers depend on mindful listening. Examples include 911 operators, teachers, and veterinarians.

Once a Day

Resist the urge to immediately answer a question from a child or colleague. Take the time to reflect and develop a thoughtful response.

Connecting to the Curriculum

Journal Writing

Encourage children to reflect on what they've learned about mindful listening and to record questions to explore at another time. They may also enjoy responding to these prompts:

- Divide your journal page into two columns. At the top of one, write "Quiet." In that column, draw or write places or events that are quiet (the library, clouds passing by, a sleeping kitten). At the top of the other column, write "Noisy" and list or draw places or events that are noisy (a firecracker, a crying baby, an airplane).

- Draw a picture of yourself by a lake, in a forest, or on a beach. List or write about the sounds you would hear if you were mindfully listening in that setting.

- What everyday sounds tell your brain everything is okay? Write down two or three sounds or events. Draw a happy face alongside. Then, list or draw sounds that tell your brain things aren't so fine. Draw a sad face next to those.

- **Pre-K & Kindergarten:** Have children find and cut out pictures of things that make sounds. As a group, sort the pictures into "Loud" and "Soft" sounds. Allow each child to select a picture, glue it into their journal, and dictate words that describe the sound of that object.

MATH
Multiplication's a Song

What to Do
Practice rhythmic skip counting to introduce children to patterns of repeated addition. Make up your own rhythm or song for each multiple (e.g., set each group of multiples to familiar tunes, such as singing the multiples of six to "The Itsy Bitsy Spider") or find ideas online by searching for "skip-counting songs." Show children how to raise a finger each time they sing a multiple so that they can see how many times they've added or "skipped."

What to Say
I know a way we can add really quickly! When we add the same number again and again, like 2 plus 2 plus 2, we can skip over that number of spaces on the number line and land on the right answers, just as if we did it the long way—on our fingers or by adding each time .... Let's first practice skipping or jumping on the number line by twos and then we'll try singing the numbers we land on when we keep adding 2.

Why It's Important
When you attach new information, such as math facts, to a pattern children know, you create an enjoyable, easy-to-learn mnemonic device—you are building on an existing neural network. Once memorized, the familiar tune will help them retrieve the new information.

LANGUAGE ARTS
Stories Full of Sound

What to Do
Choose a favorite story and have children brainstorm several sounds they can make when they hear recurring words or phrases, such as a character's name, a repeated line of dialogue, or an action that's repeated, such as walking through the woods. Have them make the appropriate sound every time they hear a word or phrase on your list.

What to Say
Let's imagine we can hear everything that happens in this story. What kinds of sounds would we hear? Let's try to make each sound on our list. ...When you hear me say the name of each sound, you make that sound.

Why It's Important
Listening for specific sound cues in a narrative not only sharpens focusing skills, it also connects children more closely to the text, because they are providing sensory context for the words. This enhances their comprehension of the story.

by Jan Slepian and Ann Seidler

SCIENCE
Matching Sounds

What to Do
Create sound canisters using ten to twelve clean yogurt containers or similar containers. Select materials that will make different noises when shaken in the containers, such as sand, paper clips, cotton balls, coins, eraser caps, and so forth. Make five or six pairs of sound canisters by filling pairs of containers with the same amount of one of the materials. Tape all lids securely shut. Ask children to shake the canisters gently and match the ones that make the same sounds. For easy and immediate feedback, label the bottoms of matching canisters with identical stamps, symbols, or numbers.

What to Say
Each of these sound canisters is filled with something that makes noise when you shake it. If you shake each one and listen carefully, you'll hear a sound that is different from most of the others, but the same as one of the others. Can you find the ones that go together?

Why It's Important
Matching the distinct sounds builds auditory discrimination skills which in turn support phonemic awareness.

SOCIAL-EMOTIONAL LEARNING
Who Said That?

What to Do
Help children use word choice and tone in dialogue to identify characters and feelings. Select several phrases of dialogue from a book you've read aloud. Ask children to listen to the words, then name the speaker and explain why they think he or she would say these words. For more advanced learners, repeat the phrase with a different tone of voice and invite them to reinterpret the words and feelings.

What to Say
Listen closely to the words I say. You've already heard them from one of our story characters. Be ready to tell me who you think the speaker is and why you think he or she is saying this. How do you think the character is feeling? Now I'll read it differently. How does the message of the words change?

Why It's Important
When children can distinguish different voices in their reading, they are not only able to access and enjoy texts at a more sophisticated level, they are building skills for understanding nuances of interaction among characters and, by extension, among people in real life.

Literature Link
The Cat Who Wore a Pot on Her Head
by Jan Slepian and Ann Seidler (1980). New York: Scholastic.

Little cat Bendomelina, in an attempt to drown out family noise, wears a pot on her head. A hilarious set of misadventures ensues as a result of Bendomelina's unfocused listening.

Connect this book to mindful listening and being aware of how our environment can help or hinder our ability to focus.

More Books to Share

Grimes, Nikki. (2000). *Shoe Magic.* New York: Scholastic

Showers, Paul. (1993). *The Listening Walk.* New York: HarperCollins

Wise, Margaret Brown. (1993). *Bunny's Noisy Book.* New York: HarperCollins.

the Optimistic classroom™ library

Mindful Seeing

What Is Mindful Seeing?

Crimson or ruby? Ovoid or oblong? Smile or smirk? Our ability to visually distinguish precise details has given rise to a very rich and precise descriptive vocabulary. Mindful seeing enables us to better observe ourselves, other people, and our surroundings to more fully enjoy and learn from them.

Why Practice Mindful Seeing?

As with mindful listening, mindful seeing helps children sharpen their focus by calling on one sense to very purposefully observe an object. This lesson also takes advantage of children's natural visual curiosity about people and things in their environment—and their desire to share their observations.

As children practice mindful seeing exercises, children become increasingly attuned to observing details by slowing down and focusing their attention. We can build on these skills of observation by encouraging children to apply their curiosity and perceptiveness to their academic work. In fact, sharpening visual discrimination skills can help improve skills critical in almost any subject area; for example, when children are using phonics skills to decode a word. And in the area of social-emotional learning, these skills can be tied to reading social cues and acting perceptively in response to the facial expressions and body language of others.

What Can You Expect to Observe?

"First graders are so excited when they begin to look closely and thoroughly at something. They want to talk about and compare what they've noticed afterward. I repeat mindful seeing exercises regularly as a way to help them practice both focusing attention and building analytical and descriptive skills."

—First-grade teacher

Linking to Brain Research

Emotions Shape Behavior and Learning

The amygdala, that reactive watchdog of the brain, elicits the same fear response for perceived danger as genuine danger. The behavior of a child who feels unsafe, threatened, inadequate, judged, or vulnerable to ridicule is driven by his or her brain's reaction to threat. Children who feel continually "on alert" are unable to engage in mindful behavior because their amygdala blocks incoming stimuli from reaching the rational prefrontal cortex.

The brain gives priority to emotions because they matter. Emotions are associated with the places and people in children's lives. Children who learn to associate school with a feeling of safety become confident enough to move out of their comfort zone. They feel safe expressing their ideas, working together, asking questions, and trying new things—even if it means making mistakes. You might say they train their amygdala to remain calm, keeping the information pathways to their higher brain open. And the more a child feels safe at school, the stronger those neural pathways become. The chains of neurons that result in a feeling of safety become more efficient, passing the message along faster.

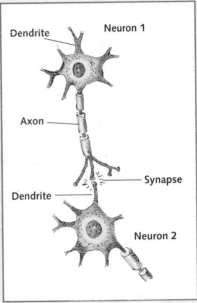

Neurons connect axon to dendrite, passing messages along via gap-jumping electrochemical exchanges called synapses.

Clarify for the Class

Model how chains of neurons pass messages. Review the parts of a nerve cell (see page 43) and tell children that this time their whole body is going to be a neuron: left hands are dendrites, which receive messages; torsos are the cell bodies; right arms are message-shuttling axons; right hands are the nerve endings that transfer messages to the next neuron's dendrites (left hand). Choose a "message" to pass, such as a coin, eraser, pebble, or other small object. The first in a lined-up chain of "neurons" then passes the message from its nerve ending (right hand) to a dendrite (left hand) of the adjacent neuron, which shuttles it across its axon to its nerve ending (right hand) where it sends it on to another neuron's dendrites, and so on until the message is received by the final neuron.

Discuss: Do you think passing the coin or other "message" would get faster with practice? How is that like what happens in the brain?

Getting Ready

What Might Happen If...?
A teacher encourages her students to make predictions before mixing the colors in the water.

GOALS

- Children practice focusing their attention on an object and describe the visual details they observe.
- Children strengthen their visual vocabulary and memory through mindful seeing.

MATERIALS

- chart paper
- objects that can be classified by color, texture, shape, and size
- one or more large, clear containers (such as a large fish bowl)
- liquid watercolor or food dye (blue, red, yellow)
- eyedropper
- (optional) Sensory Web activity sheet (p. 155)

CREATING THE OPTIMISTIC CLASSROOM

Supporting English Language Learners Making ELLs feel welcome and safe to participate with fluent English speakers is critical to helping them prime their brains for learning. Children in the early stages of learning English have few oral skills, but they are listening closely in an attempt to figure out what is happening around them. These children may be quiet, but they are absorbing information. They will pick up language related to concrete classroom activities first, such as "Draw a picture" or "Gather around my desk." Use gestures with these common classroom instructions to help your observant ELLs attach meaning to the words.

Eye-Catching Swirls
The changing colors and
movement of food coloring
drops in water are a visual
treat that keeps young
children focused.

MINDUP Warm-Up

Seeing Red, Seeing Soft

Guide children in looking at the world around them and building their vocabulary to
describe what they see. Before class begins, "salt" the classroom with objects that
children will be able to classify by color, shape, texture, and size. These can be a
combination of objects that are already in the room and ones that you bring in.

Begin the activity by asking children which part of the body they use to look at
the world around them. Then have them focus on identifying objects with specific
characteristics, for example: "I see red. What could I be looking at?" "I see a circle.
What could I be looking at?" "I see soft. What could I be looking at?" "I see tiny.
What could I be looking at?"

PRE-K CORNER: Use color and shape cards to reinforce descriptive words, such as *red*
and *square*. The cards will also help ELLs build vocabulary.

Use a T-chart to record the category and corresponding objects that children identify
and name. Let older children and proficient writers share scribing responsibility.

Discuss: We discovered a lot of different things in our classroom today. How did you
know without touching it that the stuffed bear was soft? How did you know without
measuring it that the button was tiny?

Leading the Lesson

Water Magic

Engage

Explore

What to Do

Review primary and secondary colors with children. Connect the hunt for specific colors, shapes, textures, and sizes in the warm-up exercise to mindful seeing. Set the lesson goal of focusing on an object and describing visual details.

- Today, we're going to look more closely at colors and how they change.

- In an experiment, a scientist often uses mindful seeing to learn information. We're going to do an experiment with colors and water.

PRE-K CORNER: Focus on the concepts of color and change with younger children. Skip the discussion of experiments.

Fill a large, clear container (a large fish bowl or the top of a water cooler) with warm water. Place it on a desk or table and gather children around it. Using an eyedropper, drop at least six drops of blue food dye or liquid water color into the container.

- Watch carefully. What color did I put into the water? What is happening to the color? Look at the shape. What does it look like? (I see a mushroom.) See how the shape is changing? The color is still moving through the water. What do you see now? How has the color changed?

Record children's observations on chart paper or on a display copy of the Sensory Web activity sheet. Repeat the experiment for the remaining primary colors. (Fill another container with warm water or empty and refill the first container.) Then create "magic water" for the secondary colors; mix red and blue for purple, yellow and blue for green, and red and yellow for orange.

- What happens when I mix red and blue? How are both colors moving through the water? What happens when I stir the colors together? What color do you see now?

Why It's Important

Mindful seeing is one of a scientist's greatest tools. Careful observation using all the senses is crucial to the success of an investigative experiment.

Watching the movement of color through the water is magical to children, as is the creation of the secondary colors. They've learned the mindful behavior of a scientist and the importance of doing experiments.

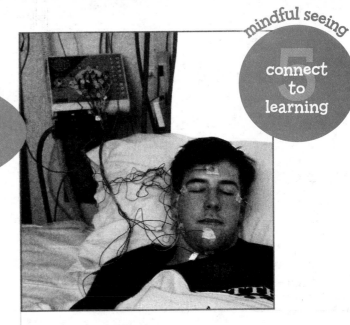

Reflect

Talk to children about the "magic water" experiment and about how they used their eyes to observe.

* What did you see when I put each color into the water?

* What did you see when I put two colors into the water?

* What if we didn't have any purple paint? What could we do?

Compare mindful seeing to mindful listening.

* Remember when we listened as mindfully as we could to different sounds? Today, we used mindful seeing to look at colors. Which was easier for you to do: mindful listening or mindful seeing?

Have children think about how mindful seeing helps them (or could help them) in different situations.

* Think about mindful seeing. How could it help you every day? How could mindful seeing help you on your way to school? How could it help you get along with other people?

To encourage children to apply some of the observation and descriptive skills they've developed in this lesson, they need to realize that they can benefit from mindful seeing in daily life. Help them generate ideas about the benefits, including using examples from your own experience (e.g., looking for a lost shoe, knowing when a friend is mad or sad, observing the pattern on a turtle's shell).

MINDUP
In the Real World

Career Connection

What do waves have to do with sleep? If you're a sleep technologist—everything! By monitoring instruments that measure a sleeping patient's brain, eye movements, muscle activity, and heart rhythm, the technologist charts sleep stages and identifies problems that may affect a person's sleep. Technologists receive input from 12 different channels and 22 wire attachments to the patient. While keeping an eye on the patients, technologists must also continuously monitor an array of electronic equipment. Only an experienced technologist can read and interpret the wave patterns that flow across the computer screen.

Discuss: Why might mindful seeing be an important skill if you're a referee or a teacher? Who else might need to use mindful seeing to do a job well?

Once a Day

Choose two similar assignments to scrutinize, such as prewriting exercises done several days apart. Use mindful seeing to observe areas of growth. Review with children what you've noticed so they can build on these improvements.

Connecting to the Curriculum

Journal Writing

Encourage children to reflect on what they've learned about mindful seeing and to record questions to explore at another time. They may also enjoy responding to these prompts:

- Colors can represent feelings. Someone who is angry might "see red." How are you feeling right now—sad, mad, glad? Use one or more colors to show that feeling. Ask a classmate how the color(s) make him or her feel.

- What do you see on your way to your classroom in the morning? Use words and pictures to describe at least three things you see.

- Close your eyes. Think of something that is enormous. Then think of something that is tiny. Write about or draw what you saw in your mind.

- **Pre-K & Kindergarten:** Ask children to study their faces in a mirror for 10–15 seconds. Then have them draw a picture of their faces. Encourage them to verbalize one or two details that describe color, shape, texture, or size in their drawings. Scribe those details in children's journals.

SCIENCE
Cloud Pictures

What to Do
Take children outside on a cloudy day. Find a location where everyone can look at the clouds. As children study the clouds, share some information about why clouds are important. Then have them tell what kinds of pictures they see in the clouds; for example, a cloud may look like a soft, puffy rabbit. Point out how the cloud pictures change. Let older children fill in the Sensory Web Activity sheet to describe what they observe about the clouds.

What to Say
The clouds in the sky bring us rain and snow. They turn gray and black when a storm is coming. Clouds are fascinating to watch. I see a cloud that looks like a boat sailing through the sky. Do you see it, too? Clouds move and change. My cloud doesn't look like a boat anymore. What cloud pictures do you see? How does your cloud change? What do you think makes cloud shapes change?

Why It's Important
Mindfully observing clouds can give children clues about the weather. Those observations can affect the choices they make, such as deciding which clothes to wear and whether to play indoors or outdoors. Noticing cloud pictures gives children the vocabulary to talk about and describe the different types of clouds.

MATH
Searching for Shapes

What to Do
Lead children in a treasure hunt for two- and three-dimensional shapes inside and outside the classroom. Ask them to bring notebooks and pencils to list or draw their findings. Take a set of shape flash cards with you for children to review. Model the discovery of a shape in the surroundings and verify your discovery using the flash cards.

What to Say
Shapes are all around us; the more we look around us for shapes, the more shapes we'll see. This flash card shows a triangle. Do you see a triangle? The yellow sign at the corner has the shape of a triangle. It has three sides, like the triangle on this flash card. Look mindfully around you. What shapes do you see?

Why It's Important
When children can identify the shapes of things around them, the concept of shapes becomes concrete. Verifying that an object has a particular shape reinforces their understanding of the attributes of each shape.

LANGUAGE ARTS/PHYSICAL EDUCATION
Observe the Word

What to Do
Introduce (or review) the words *straight, curvy, circular,* and *wavy.* Assign one of these words to pairs of children. Have each child work independently to create a dance or movement that shows the word; for example, skipping in a straight line or turning in a circle. Ask partners to share their dances and then compare and contrast their movements. Then encourage them to collaborate to create a dance or movement for the word.

What to Say
We've talked about the meanings of straight, curvy, circular, and wavy. I'm going to give one of these words to each pair. I want each partner to create a dance or movement that shows the word. Share your dances. Watch closely as your partner moves. Think about how your dances are alike and different and talk about that. Then work together to create a new dance for the word.

Why It's Important
When children share their thoughts and ideas, they must feel that they are in a safe, nonjudgmental environment. Their amygdala can't be stopping the flow of information to the rest of the brain. Mindful seeing will help children engage more deeply in the task. They'll be able to offer, and listen to, thoughtful comments.

SOCIAL-EMOTIONAL LEARNING
Every Picture Tells a Story

What to Do
Strengthen children's ability to identify and label their emotions. Select an unfamiliar picture book with illustrations that vividly portray characters and their emotions. Display the book so everyone can see the illustrations. Ask children to study each illustration, focusing on the characters' expressions and posture. Work with the class to tell the story of each picture and record it on the board. When you have finished, read the story back to the class.

What to Say
Today, we'll look at a new book. We won't read the words—we'll just look closely at each picture. At the end, we'll look at all the pictures again and retell the story. Here's the first picture. Who do you see? What is the character feeling? How can you tell?

Why It's Important
Putting names to emotions and being aware of their body's reactions help children overcome the amygdala's fight-flight-freeze. In times of intense feeling, children can learn to employ strategies to refocus their energy and calm themselves.

mindful seeing

extend the lesson

Literature Link
I Spy School Days
by Walter Wick and Jean Marzollo (1995). New York: Scholastic.

After sharing this book, children may look at their school surroundings in a more meaningful way. The spreads in this book focus on such diverse locations in the classroom and school as a blackboard, a puppet theater, and the surface of a playground. Riddles ask readers to find everything from a paper-clip chain to eight traffic cones in the accompanying photos.

Connect this book to looking more deeply at our surroundings—mindfully seeing details in the places we see every day.

More Books to Share

Golson, Terry.(2009). *Tillie Lays an Egg.* New York: Scholastic.

Rylant, Cynthia. (1998). *Tulip Sees America.* New York: Scholastic.

Tafuri, Nancy. (1997). *What the Sun Sees/What the Moon Sees.* New York: Scholastic.

the Optimistic classroom™ library

Mindful
Smelling

What Is Mindful Smelling?

Just by catching a whiff of a familiar scent, our brain can call to mind the people, places, or things we associate with it. Mindful smelling—using our sense of smell to be more aware of our environment—can help us to keenly observe our world and sharpen our memory.

Why Practice Mindful Smelling?

Practicing focused awareness with a new sense, smell, continues to broaden children's ability to observe and enjoy their experiences. As they slow down to study and take notes on several distinct aromas during this lesson, children practice taking in new information without jumping too quickly to judgment—deciding, for example, that a smell is "gross" without further consideration.

By prompting them to stay with their observations, we give children an opportunity to be fully engaged in what they're doing and to reflect on their experiences, which bolsters their sense of self-awareness and self-control. In this lesson, children also discover how memories and important information can be attached to and triggered by smells, because the smell and memory centers in the brain are close to each other, providing another tool for learning new material as well as recognizing and regulating emotional responses that may be triggered by a sense memory.

What Can You Expect to Observe?

"Scents are one of the hardest sensory experiences for children to describe. Scent exploration is especially helpful for practicing mindfulness because children really have to pause and make connections to the mystery scents—coming up with a word or an experience that reminds them of the smell. Working with scent descriptions has been a great vocabulary-builder."

—Second-grade teacher

Linking to Brain Research

Dopamine: The Chemistry of Pleasure and Reward

Our brains have more than four dozen types of neurotransmitters, chemicals that allow signals to pass between neurons. One of these neurotransmitters, dopamine, plays a role in producing and regulating positive feelings such as pleasure, hopefulness, optimism, and keen interest. When we have sufficient levels of this "feel-good" neurotransmitter in our brain, we are more able to maintain motivation, delay gratification, and feel rewarded and content. As levels of dopamine in the brain change, so does our outlook on life.

Dopamine release is triggered during pleasure-inducing experiences including smelling and eating a favorite food, seeing friends, enjoying sports, solving a puzzle, and accomplishing a task. Studies show that students who learn at a young age to connect the "feel-good" times with positive behaviors are better able to access the self-soothing, internal reward system that comes as standard equipment in every human brain. As those students mature, they are less likely to seek the dopamine surges that come with high-risk behaviors like drugs, alcohol, promiscuity, reckless driving, and overeating. In fact, young people who consistently feel pleasure and reward during sports, music, theater, dance, art, social interaction, and positive classroom experiences are not as likely to be involved in risky behaviors.

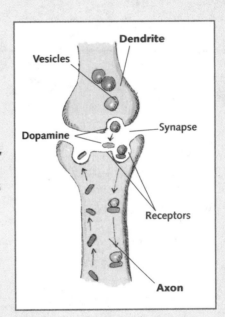

When a dopamine release is triggered, vesicles in the dendrites empty their dopamine and receptors in the axon of the receiving cell are activated to pass the message forward, across the synapse.

Clarify for the Class

Feeling good is important for learning. Explain that positive feelings help our brains remember, concentrate, pay attention, and keep trying. We can create positive feelings in ourselves by doing things that give us pleasure and a feeling of accomplishment. Sports, music, art, talking to friends, and joining in during class are all good ways to feel your best and gain confidence in yourself.

Discuss: What makes you feel better? Can you give an example of a time when you felt better after doing these activities?

Getting Ready

That's Not Water!
Children focus on their sense of smell to distinguish among several clear liquids.

GOALS
- Children focus their attention through their sense of smell and describe their observations.
- Children identify thoughts and feelings triggered by various scents.

MATERIALS
- chart paper and marker
- 2 sets of small opaque containers with lids, (e.g., film canisters)
- at least four familiar scents (e.g., pine needles, vinegar, vanilla, cinnamon sticks or bark, baby powder, dried bacon bits, orange juice)
- scratch paper or Sounds & Scents activity sheet (p. 154)

PREPARATION TIPS
- Place the scent samples in containers (for liquid scents, use saturated cotton balls). Label each container on the bottom. Create a reference key.

CREATING THE OPTIMISTIC CLASSROOM
Brain-Inspired Instruction One crucial factor that impacts dopamine levels in children is the mood of their teacher! Remember that it is important for you to maintain healthy levels of dopamine. To keep your own brain working at its best:
- Consciously focus on the good things that are happening in your classroom.
- Allow yourself to laugh with children.
- Be realistic about the goals you set.
- Celebrate your own successes with children.

Common Scents
Even familiar scents like vanilla, cocoa, and baby powder can prove tricky for students who rely primarily on their vision to process sensory input.

MINDUP Warm-Up

Scent Memory Practice

Tell children that their brains can remember their favorite food, even before they see it, by just catching a whiff of it. Their sense of smell can sharpen their focus, and scents can help them build and recall memories.

Point out that different places have different smells, too. The grocery store has different smells from the laundromat.

Write on chart paper or the board (leave blanks for the underlined words):

	Example:
I like the smells at [place].	I like the smells at <u>the park</u>.
I smell [one or more scents].	I smell <u>hot dogs and flowers</u>.
It reminds me of [memory].	It reminds me of <u>summer</u>.

Encourage children to shut their eyes and think of a favorite place and then to remember the smells there. Read aloud each sentence. Ask older children to write or draw their responses on a sheet of paper and then share them with the class.

PRE-K CORNER: Suggest a specific place that will be familiar to all children, such as the school cafeteria or art room. Scribe their responses.

Discuss: Think of an important event in your life. What smell, or scent, do you remember? What happens when you smell that scent?

Leading the Lesson

Mystery Scents

Engage

What to Do

Build background for the lesson by making connections to previous mindful sensing exercises. Introduce the concept of mindful smelling.

- We know now that another word for a *smell* is a *scent*. A *scent* is the smell someone or something gives off.

- Think about the scent of a flower. What words could you use to describe that scent or smell?

- Think about the scent of pizza. What words could you use to describe how it smells?

PRE-K CORNER: With younger children, expect to hear *yummy, yucky, icky,* and other terms. Accept those terms as you expand their vocabulary.

Explain to children that they will do an activity that will help them develop mindful smelling.

Explore

What to Do

Put the same color dots on containers with matching smells and create a key. Organize the class into two groups and have each group pull their chairs into a circle. Explain the following procedure: You will give each group a container with the same mystery smell. Without talking, each child will sniff the smell for several seconds and then pass the container to the next child. (Give a signal, such as a tap of a finger cymbal, when it's time to pass the container.)

Assure children that this is a safe activity and that their amygdala, their security guard, should pass on information about the smell to their prefrontal cortex, their wise leader, without making faces or sounds.

- What does this scent make you think of?

- Does it remind you of being in a particular place or with a particular person?

- What words would you use to describe this scent?

- What do you think the scent is?

Record children's responses on the Mystery Sound/Scent activity sheet. Reveal the scent when children are stumped. Follow the same procedure for each set of scents.

Why It's Important

As with mindful listening and mindful seeing exercises, concentrating on using a single sense to identify details helps children prime their RAS to gather lots of information from their environment that they might not have otherwise noticed. Trying to identify the smells around them gets children focused on taking cues from their noses.

By setting clear expectations for their behavior, children can focus on the new experience of smelling "mystery" scents in a way that focuses their attention.

From the Research
Any pleasurable activity used even as a brief break
can give the amygdala a chance to "cool down"
and the neurotransmitters time to rebuild as the
students are refreshed.
(Kato & McEwen, 2003)

Reflect

Pass around each scent sample again. Ask children
whether any of the scents triggered a memory and, if
so, suggest they share the memory with a partner.

- Did any of the smells make you think about a
person, place, an experience, or a feeling? Share
that memory with a partner.

- Which part of the brain helped you store that
scent memory? That's right, the hippocampus is
our memory saver.

- Did you like some smells more than others? Share
with a partner the smells you prefer.

Help children see mindful smelling as a focusing tool.

- Like mindful listening and mindful seeing,
mindful smelling helps us focus our attention.

- Smell is an important sense. It helps us recognize
and learn about the world around us.

- Scents can remind us of memories.

As children begin to focus on and distinguish smells,
they are building their scent vocabulary with words,
such as *sweet, strong, mild, rotten, fruity, spicy, sour,
perfumey,* and *fishy*. The addition of mindful smelling
adds to the strategies they can use to become sharper
thinkers and make better choices.

MINDUP
In the Real World

Career Connection

Do you have a nose for rocks? If you have
a keen sense of smell, your nose may lead
you to a career in geology. Geologists
identify rocks and minerals by relying on
a range of sensory input that sometimes
includes smell. That's because certain
rocks and minerals have a distinct odor.
Sniffing a rock and breathing deeply and
mindfully can help geologists detect, for
example, sulfur (smells like rotten eggs),
shale (smells like mud), and arsenic (smells
like garlic). In fact, Japanese scientists are
researching the smell of the moon—in this
way they hope to identify the minerals
that make up the moon's surface.

Discuss: What's your favorite cooking
smell and why? How would a chef, a
professional cook, or a baker use mindful
smelling to do his or her job?

Once a Day

Add a mindful smelling cue to children's
Core Practice, such as, "As you breathe
in, be aware of classroom scents in the air
around you."

Connecting to the Curriculum

Mindful smelling supports children's connection to their own learning process and to the content areas and literature.

Journal Writing

Encourage children to reflect on what they've learned about mindful smelling and to record questions to explore at another time. They may also enjoy responding to these prompts:

- On a sheet of paper, write the names of the four seasons: FALL, WINTER, SPRING, SUMMER. Leave room underneath each name to write and/or draw at least three smells that you remember from each season.

- Think of a time when your sense of smell warned your amygdala, your brain's security guard, of danger. Use that memory to draw a safety poster.

- These animals can't see very well, but they have a well-developed sense of smell: bats, bears, rhinos, and moles. Write a story about one of these animals and the importance of its sense of smell. Focus on the scents that your animal character smells.

- **Pre-K & Kindergarten:** Ask children to identify their favorite smell. Encourage them to think of five words to show how this smell makes them feel and what memories it triggers.

SCIENCE
A Mindful Match

What to Do
Use the two sets of containers you used in the warm-up activity. (You may want to change the color coding on the containers in case children were mindfully observing the colors in the lesson.) Challenge children to sniff the scent in one of the containers and then use mindful smelling to find the container with the matching scent. Encourage them to talk about how mindful smelling helped them complete the task.

What to Say
Remember these containers from the lesson? Both sets of containers contain the same scents. Sniff one container in this set. Which container in the other set has the same scent? Use mindful smelling to find the container with the same scent. Tell me how you used mindful smelling to match the smells.

Why It's Important
Children have to rely solely on their noses in this activity, which helps them strengthen their ability to mindfully smell. In describing how they used mindful smelling, children continue to develop their scent vocabulary and tap into their scent memories.

LANGUAGE ARTS
The Nose Knows

What to Do
Assemble pairs of foods and liquids that look similar but have very different smells, such as water and white vinegar, black coffee and vanilla extract, and a slice of peeled potato and a slice of peeled apple. Display each food in a transparent container with a lid. Ask children to identify the foods. Then have them use mindful smelling to confirm or change their identifications.

What to Say
Look at these containers. What do you see? Which containers look like they go together? Look closely at each pair of containers. What do you see? Are the foods the same? Now open one pair of containers. How are the scents alike or different? What do you think you are smelling?

Why It's Important
Children learn to use more than one sense to make and confirm predictions. The senses are interrelated and work together; however, one may provide more accurate information than another.

the Optimistic™ classroom journal

ART
Scratch and Sniff

What to Do
Explain the concept of scratch and sniff: A surface, such as the page of a book, is coated with a scent; when it's scratched, the scent, which is usually related to an image under the coating, is released. Select one of the children's favorite read-aloud books. Ask them to explain where they would place a scratch-and-sniff patch and what scent would be released.

What to Say
Have you ever smelled a scratch-and-sniff card? When you scratch the picture on the card, you can smell a scent. For example, if you scratched the drawing of a rose on a birthday card, you would smell a sweet, rosy smell. Let's look at one of our favorite books and decide which pictures would be good for scratch and sniff. Which scent should we use for each scratch-and-sniff picture?

Why It's Important
In picture books, the artist tries to enhance the writer's words. The images unfolding across the pages give children, no matter their reading level or their familiarity with the language, an entry into the story. Thinking about how to incorporate smells into the illustrations of a picture book deepens children's sensory experience with the text.

SOCIAL-EMOTIONAL LEARNING
A World of Scents

What to Do
Duplicate these sentences for each child:

I smell my _____ (familiar object from home).
It makes me feel _____.
It makes me think about _____ (memory).
These words describe the smell: _____.

Ask children to use the frame to describe a familiar object.

What to Say
There are scents that we smell every day, without really noticing them. Choose a familiar object and smell it as mindfully as you can. How does the smell make you feel? What does it make you think of? Which words describe the smell?

Why It's Important
It may take some practice for children to relax their amygdala's grip on reactions to different smells. This activity will help children appreciate familiar scents and understand that a different smell is not a "funny" smell.

Literature Link
The Story of Ferdinand

by Munro Leaf
(2010). New York: Scholastic.

In this classic book, first published more than 60 years ago, you'll meet a bull unlike any other. Gentle Ferdinand prefers to sit under his favorite tree and smell the flowers rather than fight. Connect this to a discussion of individual preferences and smells that are calming and pleasurable.

More Books to Share

Hyde, Margaret. (2009). *Mo Smells Green: A Scentsational Journey*. Winnetka, CA: Mo's Nose LLC.

Meacham Rau, D. (2005). *Sniff, Sniff: A Book about Smell*. Mankato, MN: Picture Window Books.

Perkins, Al. (1970). *The Nose Book*. New York: Random House Children's Books.

the Optimistic classroom™ library

Mindful
Tasting

What Is Mindful Tasting?

To fully appreciate the food we eat—whether it's a complex treat, such as sweet grilled corn with hot chili and sour lime or a simple bowl of oatmeal—requires mindful tasting, or slowing down to savor our food and notice its flavor, texture, and temperature.

Why Practice Mindful Tasting?

Eating is something that is hardly ever done mindfully by young people. This makes mindful tasting a valuable task for demonstrating mindful awareness. A simple exercise of savoring and describing a morsel of food helps children understand the changes that can occur when an everyday act is performed slowly and with conscious attention to the experience.

Mindful tasting helps children identify discrete taste sensations, build descriptive skills, and approach food with a healthy outlook. It may even make them connect healthful eating to success at schoolwork and interactions in the classroom. The exercise cues children to think carefully about what they're tasting and supports good digestion as they chew slowly and deliberately. With practice, children may be willing to try foods that are not part of their usual diet and make healthy food choices. Key social-emotional outcomes are building self-regulation skills and being accepting of new foods, which may lay the foundation for tolerance of cultural traditions outside of one's own.

What Can You Expect to Observe?

"Pre-K children really get a kick out of making each bite of food a new discovery. They also learn how slowing down and chewing well can help them enjoy their food even more. We often bring mindful eating into our snack and lunch time, and children now take more time to eat and digest. This lesson starts them on the path of healthy eating habits."

—Pre-K teacher

Linking to Brain Research

Relaxed and Alert:
The Role of Neurotransmitters

Neurotransmitters are key to the dynamic and ever-changing ecosystem of our brain. These chemical messengers influence a wide range of feelings and behaviors and are affected by sensory input and general health. Stress—real or perceived—causes changes in levels of neurotransmitters, including these three:

- Dopamine plays a crucial role in motivation, pleasure, and addiction and influences paying attention, planning, and moving the body.
- Serotonin contributes to the regulation of appetite, sleep, aggression, mood, and pain.
- Norepinephrine is important for attentiveness, emotions, sleeping, dreaming, and learning.

Increases and/or decreases in the level of one or more of these neurotransmitters affect our mental state and the feelings and behaviors generated by it. Attentiveness, engagement, competence, and achievement are only possible when a learner's brain is in a receptive state, allowing for a calm and mindful response. Mindful tasting, like mindful listening, seeing and smelling, gives children an opportunity to be both relaxed and aware. The novelty of this activity, along with children's curiosity and engagement, helps balance neurotransmitters and produce a relaxed, yet very alert, state of mind. Mindful activities help train the prefrontal cortex to pay attention, absorb details, and think clearly.

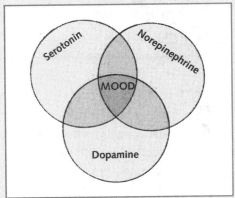

Levels and combinations of the neurotransmitters serotonin, norepinephrine, and dopamine influence our mental state.

Clarify for the Class

Can mindful tasting help us compare real and fake flavors? Find out by mindfully tasting candy versus fruit. Choose comparable flavors, like an orange slice and an orange-flavored jellybean or a banana and banana-flavored taffy. Have children sample both, taking their time to savor each.

Discuss: In what ways did the candy and fruit taste the same? What tastes, textures, or smells were different?

Getting Ready

Can You Resist This Morsel?
A teacher encourages children to slow down and use all their senses to appreciate their morsel.

GOALS

* Children will focus on savoring a morsel of food and describe their experience.
* Children will identify ways that mindful tasting can help them eat healthily.

MATERIALS

* food morsels (one per child): marshmallows, grapes, mini pretzels, and chocolate chips (Wear gloves or tongs to distribute the morsels.)
* grocery store circulars
* chart paper

PREPARATION TIPS

* Be aware of any food allergies students may have and avoid high-risk foods, such as nuts.
* Be sure to have children wash their hands before the lesson, which involves putting food in their mouths.

CREATING THE OPTIMISTIC CLASSROOM

Brain-Inspired Instruction Create a visual chart to help children associate taste- and eating-related words with familiar foods. Here's a sampling: *sweet, spicy, salty, crispy, sticky, chewy, crunchy, slimy, smooth, bitter, sour, juicy, dry, tough, nutty, creamy, soft, hard.* On a large sheet of chart paper, write the descriptive words. Ask children if they know any of them. Encourage them to look through grocery store circulars for examples of food to paste beside each word, such as a banana for *sweet*. The more visual cues children have, the better they will be able to access and use the terms.

A Close Examination
As children smell and look closely at their morsel, they practice self-regulation skills.

MINDUP Warm-Up

Mindful Tasting Practice

Remind children that they have been learning how to use each of their senses in a more mindful way.

- *We have practiced mindful listening, mindful seeing, and mindful smelling. Let's practice using all these senses. Now close your eyes. Imagine that someone is cooking a big, juicy hamburger. Let your hippocampus bring up memories.*
- *What do you hear? What sounds does the meat make as it cooks?*
- *What do you see? What is the cook putting on the hamburger?*
- *What do you smell? What scents are rising from the hamburger?*
- *Now imagine taking a bite of the hamburger.*
- *What do you taste? Besides the meat, what is on the hamburger?*
- *Turn and talk to your partner. Share what you heard, saw, smelled, and tasted.*

Then ask children to talk about how their bodies responded to the mindful practice.

Discuss: What memory did you think of? How did your body change as you used your senses? Are you hungry now? What would happen if I put a plate of food in front of you? Would you eat it very fast? Or would you eat each bite slowly?

Leading the Lesson

Soft as a Marshmallow

Engage

Explore

What to Do

Introduce the concept of mindful tasting.

- Our bodies need three things: air to breathe, water to drink, and food to eat. We are used to breathing, drinking, and eating, so sometimes we don't pay attention to them. We don't notice how water or food feels on our tongue. We don't focus on how they change in our mouth.

- Today, we're going to learn how to taste mindfully. We're going to train our brains to focus on what we eat and how we eat.

- When we practiced mindful smelling, we experimented with scents. Today, we're going to do an experiment with small pieces of food.

Help children feel comfortable and safe with this lesson. Guide them in taking slow, deep breaths to calm their amygdala and prepare to be mindful.

Arrange children in a circle on the floor or at their desks. Place a piece of marshmallow in each child's palm. Write the word *marshmallow* on chart paper.

- Notice the color, shape, and texture of this food.

Tell children to close their eyes and focus on smell.

- Do you know this scent? What does it remind you of? How would you describe it?

Guide children through mindful tasting.

- Carefully put the food in your mouth. Don't bite down! Try as hard as you can to focus on how the food feels in your mouth.

- Use your tongue to move it around in your mouth. Does it feel soft? Hard?

- Bite down very slowly. How does the food taste? Is it sour? Sweet? Chew slowly and then swallow.

Write children's responses on chart paper. Repeat with the remaining morsels.

Why It's Important

Children's familiarity with mindful listening, seeing, and smelling will help prepare them to participate in this lesson. Their prefrontal cortex will be working to notice the details gathered by the RAS. Children will further develop their ability to become both relaxed and aware.

When children consciously look at and smell food before tasting it, they begin to more deeply experience the taste. They focus on appearance, texture, smell, and taste. The variety of foods sampled in this lesson gives children a basis for comparison and strengthens their tasting and food vocabularies.

Reflect

Talk about children's responses to their mindful tasting practice.

- What did you notice about your bodies as your mindfully tasted the food?

Ask children to compare the way they tasted the food in this lesson to how they usually eat their food.

- Remember when we imagined someone cooking a hamburger? Suppose we did that activity again and that afterward I gave you a whole marshmallow. How could you use mindful tasting to eat it?

Reveal that it takes 10 to 15 minutes for the stomach to send the signal to the brain that it's full.

- If we gulp down our food, we don't really taste it. If we eat too fast, we will probably eat too much. Tasting mindfully can help us enjoy our food more and make us healthier.

The regular practice of mindful tasting can have a significant effect on children's health. Not only does it have calming and focusing benefits, but it can also assist with how well children digest their food and feel satisfied, which can prevent overeating. Further, the novelty of this tasting activity can encourage children to try out new and healthful morsels.

MINDUP
In the Real World

Career Connection

Have professional taste buds, will report for work—that is, if you're a taste tester! Food scientists, who whip up all sorts of concoctions—from snack foods to beverages to condiments such as ketchup—conduct tests to comply with the standards and regulations that govern taste, texture, moisture, color, and nutrients as well as salt, fat, and sugar content. In order to meet quality controls, they rely on mindful tasters, who know how to use their tongues and taste buds to slowly, mindfully take in the full taste of every product. Taste testers might sample several dozen products and use a complicated scale to rate their choices.

Discuss: What's your favorite taste? How do you feel when you experience it? If you could be a taste-tester, where would you like to work?

Once a Day

Instead of multitasking through lunch, take at least ten minutes to really taste (and digest) your food. You'll feel more satisfied, more able to focus, and more prepared to effectively manage the needs of your day.

Connecting to the Curriculum

Journal Writing

Encourage children to reflect on what they've learned about mindful tasting and to record questions to explore at another time. They may also enjoy responding to these prompts:

- Turn today into a holiday in honor of a favorite food, such as National Pretzel Day. Draw or find a picture of the food. Then describe what this food tastes like and why it deserves its own holiday.

- How could you help your family practice mindfully eating a meal together? Write or draw a menu. Think about the taste, color, and texture of the foods and how they will go together.

- Is there a food that you've never eaten before but would like to try? What makes you curious about this food? How would you use mindful eating to try this new food?

- **Pre-K & Kindergarten:** Ask each child to think about a favorite food. Write its name in the child's journal and ask him or her to draw a picture of it. Then copy and complete as the child dictates:
  This food looks _____.
  This food smells _____.
  This food tastes _____.

the Optimistic classroom™ journal

HEALTH/ART
Don't Gulp Your Food!

What to Do
Review the benefits of mindful tasting: it trains our prefrontal cortex to pay attention, helps us focus on and appreciate our food, tells us when we're full, helps us make better choices, and so on. Inspire children to create posters showing the principles of mindful tasting and its benefits, for example, "Look! Smell! Taste!" or "Chew Slowly! Don't Gulp!" Display the posters in the cafeteria.

What to Say
Mindful tasting uses our brain. Our amygdala passes information about a taste to the prefrontal cortex. Our PFC helps us explore the taste. It helps us put words to the taste, such as sweet or sour. Then our hippocampus stores that taste memory. When we taste mindfully, we pay attention. We know when we're full and when to stop eating. Let's create a poster showing how mindful eating helps us make good choices.

Why It's Important
In our busy lives, we tend to taste mindlessly, not mindfully. There's no gratification in this kind of eating. Practicing mindful tasting at a young age starts children on the path toward better decision making about what they put into their bodies.

LANGUAGE ARTS
A Crunchy Spin

What to Do
Depending on children's ages, create a pizza spinner with four, six, or eight equal parts. Label each with a different taste word, such as *crispy, soft, sour,* and *juicy.* Explain that when the spinner lands on a piece, they must think of a topping to match the word; for example, *crispy* topping might be fried onions.

What to Say
Let's add different kinds of toppings to change the flavor of our pizza! This pizza is divided into four (or six or eight) slices. When the spinner stops, think of a topping that goes with the word on that slice. I'll spin. What topping might make it chunky?

Why It's Important
Children build and reinforce their taste vocabulary with this activity. As the game progresses, they'll expand their thinking about what ingredients might go on a pizza.

PRE-K CORNER: Cut out pictures of ingredients to match the words on the spinner and have children choose from them.

SOCIAL STUDIES
A Bread Tasting

What to Do
Read aloud a book such as *Everybody Bakes Bread* by Norah Dooley. Prepare a short note for children to take home, explaining that your class has been reading about the different kinds of bread that people bake and eat, including corn bread and chapattis. Ask parents or caretakers to supply a sample of the family's favorite bread or a recipe for it.

What to Say
We have read about baking many different kinds of bread. When you go to the store, you may see tortillas, pita bread, corn bread, challah, and naan. What kind of bread do you eat at home? Please take this letter home and ask your family to give you a piece of that kind of bread to bring in or a recipe for it. Then we'll look at, smell, and taste the different breads.

Why It's Important
Comparing the different kinds of bread will give children the opportunity to see the similarities among the breads of various cultures and to appreciate the differences among them. It will give children the opportunity to taste new foods and practice mindful tasting.

SOCIAL-EMOTIONAL LEARNING
Meet Your Taste Buds

What to Do
Introduce children to their taste buds. Pair children. Ask them to stick out their tongue so their partner can examine it. Point out the small bumps on the surface where most of our 10,000 taste buds are. Write on the board *sweet, salty, sour,* and *bitter,* and give an example of each. Challenge children to use mindful tasting to help them taste a food they think they won't like.

What to Say
Where do you think your taste buds are located? Stick out your tongue so your partner can study it. Do you see the little bumps on your tongue? Most of your 10,000 taste buds are there. Taste buds help us taste foods that are salty, sweet, sour, or bitter. At home, practice mindful tasting with a food you think you won't like. Pay attention to what your taste buds are telling you.

Why It's Important
Children's opportunities to expand their experience with different foods may be limited. Encouraging children to use mindful tasting to explore tastes may help them become more adventurous eaters.

Literature Link
Gregory, the Terrible Eater

by Mitchell Sharmat
(1980). New York: Scholastic.

Gregory the goat *is* a terrible eater. Instead of chowing down on bottle caps or boxes as most goats do, he eats fruits and vegetables and eggs. His parents consult Dr. Ram about the problem. When Gregory does begin to eat like a goat, he goes overboard and tries to eat everything in sight.

Clearly, Gregory is not practicing mindful tasting. Use the text to engage children in a discussion about how mindful tasting can prevent someone from overeating.

More Books to Share

Arnosky, J. (2008). *Gobble It Up! A Fun Song About Eating!* New York: Scholastic.

Carle, Eric. (1994). *The Very Hungry Caterpillar.* New York: Philomel Books.

Tafolla, Carmen. (2009). *What Can You Do with a Paleta?* Berkeley, CA: Tricycle Press.

the **Optimistic** classroom™ library

Mindful
Movement I

What Is Mindful Movement?

How often are we conscious of putting weight on each part of the sole of our foot as we walk? Being alert to the sensations of the body, whether we are active or at rest, is a fundamental step in increasing mindful awareness.

Why Practice Mindful Movement?

Our body and brain are partners. We get burned and the nerve cells in our skin send a signal to our brain that registers pain. We get nervous and tense about an important test and our brain sends a signal to our body to sweat and cool down.

To move mindfully is to pay close attention to the sensations of our body when it is at rest and when it is active—the body gives us signals we can easily recognize to help us monitor physical and mental states such as exertion and stress.

In this lesson, children compare the signals their body sends after physical exertion and relaxation. They begin to learn simple self-regulation skills by controlling their breathing and heart rate. Developing an understanding of the brain-body relationship helps children become better able to identify the signals their body is sending and to manage their emotions and behaviors in response.

What Can You Expect to Observe?

"We've had fun monitoring how much 'happy heart' exercise children have had for recess and P.E. class. By feeling how fast their heart is beating and noticing how warm they feel, they're aware now of how well they've exercised their bodies. This kind of physical awareness is helping them learn how to get the physical activity their bodies need, without an adult directing them to do so."

—Kindergarten teacher

Linking to Brain Research

Cortisol, the Stress Hormone

During a period of severe or persistent threat—perceived or real—the adrenal glands release extra cortisol, a hormone. Low levels of cortisol in the brain help us remain alert, and a sudden surge of the stress hormone is important in dealing with immediate danger. However, too much cortisol for too long can harm the brain and impair thinking, memory, and learning. High cortisol levels interfere with the function of neurotransmitters and can damage the hippocampus, which makes and stores memories. Excessive cortisol can make it hard to think and remember—"going blank" during a crisis may be an example of cortisol interference.

Brains in a constant state of alert due to physical, environmental, or emotional stress can have chronically elevated cortisol levels. During the crucial early years of brain development, high cortisol levels sustained over prolonged periods can cause significant damage and result in emotional dysfunction. Twenty-first-century life brings many stressors to children at an early age: lack of downtime, parental stresses, pressures to achieve, exposure to violence, over-stimulating or noisy environments, families dealing with substance abuse, unrealistic expectations, and poverty. As children learn to mindfully regulate their own breathing and heart rate, they learn to lessen their stress level and enable a healthy emotional balance.

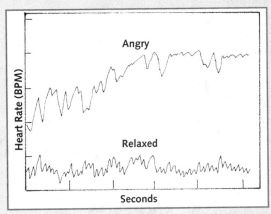

Our state of mind affects heart rate. The heart of someone who is angry can beat twice as fast as that of a relaxed person.

Clarify for the Class

Have children compare their pulses when they've been in an excited state, such as after playing a timed review game, and when they are very calm, such as after a breathing exercise. See if they can notice a difference even without a lot of movement. Explain that controlled breathing slows our heart rate.

Discuss: How do you think the controlled breathing exercise slowed our heart rate? How were our body and our mind working together?

Getting Ready

Move It!
Children touch the floor and reach for the sky to get their heart pumping.

GOALS
- Children will focus their attention on internal physical sensations, in both a relaxed and an active state.
- Children will monitor their own heart rate and exercise control over breathing and heart rate.

MATERIALS
- photo of doctor or nurse with stethoscope
- chart paper

PREPARATION TIPS
- Make space in the classroom for children to do exercises safely around their desks, or find a clear area such as the gym or an outdoor court.
- For children with special physical needs, discuss appropriate adjustments for the active part of this lesson with the P.E. teacher, nurse, and parents, as needed.

CREATING THE OPTIMISTIC CLASSROOM
Brain-Inspired Instruction When children are engaged in activities they enjoy, the amygdala relaxes, cortisol levels decrease, and positive neurotransmitters have time to rebuild. To allow the brain to return to an optimal state for learning, create a relaxed, brain-friendly classroom environment by doing the following: use limited periods for talking and listening, encourage peer-talk to cement learning, laugh with your children, and give immediate positive feedback when it is appropriate and sincere.

Feel That Beat
Following a movement activity, children
focus in on feeling for their pulse.

MINDUP Warm-Up

Practice Taking a Pulse

Display the photo. Ask children if a doctor or nurse has ever used a stethoscope to
listen to their heart. Explain that the heart is a muscle. Make a fist and squeeze it
rhythmically.

- *Imagine this is my heart. Do you see it beating?*
- *What happens when you run fast? Does your heart beat faster or slower? Show me
  with your fist.*

Tell children they are going to find their pulse and measure their heart rate.
Demonstrate and have children practice finding their pulse in either of these ways:

- Hold your hand palm up; press the index and middle finger of the other hand just
  below your palm.
- Press your index and middle finger firmly at the center of the base of your throat.

Ask children which pulse point is easier for them to locate.

PRE-K CORNER: Younger children may not be able to measure their heart rate, but
they can describe how their body feels while they mindfully relax.

Discuss: When do you feel your heart working hard? When does it slow down?

Leading the Lesson

Mindful Relaxing and Mindful Moving

Engage	Explore

What to Do

Engage

Review the process of finding a pulse (from the warm-up). Explain that our heart beats most rapidly and strongly when our body works hard and that it beats more slowly when we are relaxed.

- We're sitting comfortably. Is your heart beating fast or slowly?

Then guide children through mindful relaxing.

- We can slow down our heartbeat. We can do this by mindfully relaxing. Are you ready?

- Bring all your attention to your body and your breathing. Close your eyes. Take several deep, slow breaths. Let your PFC focus on how relaxed your arms, legs, and neck feel. Feel your slow, deep breaths fill your lungs. Feel how your shoulders relax as you slowly let out the breaths.

Guide children in finding their pulse points. On your signal, have them begin counting their heartbeats. Time them for 15 seconds. Have them share the number of heartbeats they counted. Lead them to understand that heart rates vary from person to person.

Explore

Explain to children that they will be moving from a relaxed state with a calm heart rate to an excited state with a rapid heart rate. Then guide them in the practice of mindful moving. Ask them to name fun exercises they could do in the space. List or simply sketch their suggestions on chart paper, such as jumping or running in place, and so on. Give children the following instructions:

- Choose one exercise. When I say, "Move!", do that exercise. Move until I say, "Stop!" and raise my hand.

- We'll move for about one minute. Pay close attention as you move. What is happening to your body? What is happening to your breath?

- When you stop, find your pulse point. When I say, "Count!", start counting your heart beats. Ready? Move!

Why It's Important

Engage

Mindful relaxing is one more strategy for children to use to calm themselves in stressful situations. They can count their heartbeats to determine whether their heart rate is elevated and take steps to mindfully relax.

Explore

Children experience the rise in their heart rate when they move, and they confirm the rise by counting their heart beats. As we move, our hearts have to work harder and beat more rapidly to pump oxygen-filled blood to our muscles and we're able to move with greater energy.

Reflect

Ask children to sit comfortably and talk with a partner about what they discovered about their heart rate before and after the exercise. Bring children together to discuss the experience.

- Did your heart beat faster after you did the exercise? Show me with a thumbs-up or thumbs-down gesture.

Review the changes that children experienced as their heart rate slowed.

- Sometimes, when we are upset or angry or excited, our heart rate can go up. How can we use mindful relaxing to calm down?

- When you move, your heart beats more rapidly. It's sending blood to your muscles. That helps you move more easily, with more energy.

Our brains and our bodies work in conjunction to keep us healthy and safe. When children are mindful of the signals their body sends, they can use those signals to make good decisions about their health.

MINDUP
In the Real World

Career Connection

A tai chi (tie-CHEE) instructor teaches the ancient art of "meditation in motion," which connects mind and body and promotes serenity through gentle movements. Originally developed in ancient China for self-defense, tai chi has evolved into a noncompetitive, self-paced system of postures or movements performed in a slow, mindful manner. Each posture flows into the next without pause; there are more than 100 possible movements and positions, all of them coordinated with breathing.

Discuss: Is there a special move in a sports or a gym or a dance class that you've practiced over and over? How has practice helped you become a better player or dancer?

Once a Day

Notice children's posture after they've been working for a while—how well they hold themselves upright reflects their degree of alertness. Take short breaks to allow them to move (e.g., shaking out or doing a few jumping jacks), refresh, and refocus as needed.

Connecting to the Curriculum

Mindful movement supports children's connection to their own learning process and to the content areas and literature.

Journal Writing

Encourage children to reflect on what they've learned about mindful movement and to record questions to explore at another time. They may also enjoy responding to these prompts:

- Look in magazines and books for pictures of people whose bodies are working hard. List the clues that show their bodies are hard at work.

- Create a character called the Talking Heart. Use the Talking Heart to teach people how to find their pulse and count their heart beats.

- Draw and label two pictures. One picture should show you at play. The other picture should show you at rest. Before you begin to draw, think about what happens to your body when you play and when you rest. Compare your play and rest activities with others in your class.

- **Pre-K & Kindergarten:** Ask children to name three activities that make their hearts beat more rapidly. Have them draw the activities in their journals and scribe the caption they give for each one.

SOCIAL STUDIES
The World in Motion

What to Do
Teach children global versions of familiar playtime activities, such as hopscotch and jump rope. Consult books such as *Hopscotch Around the World* by Mary D. Lankford or *Jump Rope (Games Around the World series)* by Dana Meachen Rau for variations. Point out each country's location on a globe or map. Ask children to describe how their bodies feel before, during, and after the activity.

What to Say
Children all over the world play the same games. The games are a little different in each country. Italian children play a hopscotch game called Campana. We're going to play a game of hopscotch that children in Nigeria play. Nigeria is in Africa. Here it is on the map. Before we begin, tell me how your body is feeling. Pay attention to how your body changes during the game.

Why It's Important
Children learn to recognize that there are different cultures in the world and to acknowledge and appreciate the similarities and differences among them. At the same time, they are practicing mindful movement and learning more about the responses of their own bodies to movement and to rest.

PHYSICAL EDUCATION
Mindful Walking

What to Do
Ask children to walk slowly and deliberately around the classroom or gym, focusing on how their legs and feet feel and what their arms are doing. Then have them increase their speed and repeat the process. Encourage them to compare the sensations in their bodies at the two speeds.

What to Say
We're going to practice mindful walking. Let's walk slowly around the room. As you walk, pay close attention to your body. How do your legs and feet feel? How do the other parts of your body feel? Now let's walk faster. How do your legs and feet feel now? Has the way your body feels changed?

Why It's Important
Mindful walking gives children a greater awareness of their body and the difference between various levels of exercise. They also become aware of how the different parts of their body work together and how their heart rate and breathing change with speed.

the Optimistic classroom™ journal

MUSIC
On Your Feet

What to Do
Choose a few pieces of music from different genres, such as a polka, reggae, jazz, classical, and rock. Play each piece and ask children to sit and listen for 15–20 seconds. Then encourage them to get up and move to the music for a minute or so. End the activity by asking children about their responses to each piece of music and how they changed the way they moved to each piece.

What to Say
I'm going to play a piece of music for you. It is called polka music. People enjoy dancing to it. Please sit and listen mindfully. When I give the signal, please stand up and move to the music. Continue to listen mindfully. Let the music tell your body how to move.

Why It's Important
By listening mindfully and moving mindfully to music, children pick up the differences among different genres of music. You can help a child who responds strongly to a particular piece of music learn to use it to soothe or to energize his or her mind and body.

Literature Link
Jazz on a Saturday Night

by Leo and Diane Dillon
(2007). New York: Scholastic.

The focus here is on jazz greats Ella Fitzgerald, John Coltrane, Charlie Parker, Thelonious Monk, Miles Davis, Stanley Clarke, and Max Roach. At rest or in motion, children will respond to the Dillons' rhyming text and the music on the accompanying CD.

More Books to Share

Christelow, Eileen. (2005). *Five Little Monkeys Jumping on the Bed*. New York: Scholastic.

Cohen, Arlene. (2007). *Stories on the Move: Integrating Literature and Movement with Children, from Infants to Age 14*. Santa Barbara, CA: Libraries Unlimited.

Ryder, Joanne. (1996). *Earth Dance*. New York: Henry Holt.

SOCIAL-EMOTIONAL LEARNING
Good Posture, Good Thinking

What to Do
Have children practice sitting upright, but not rigidly, with ears over shoulders, shoulders over hips, and feet flat on the floor or a block. Have children imagine that their head is a balloon, floating lightly above their shoulders. Explain that good posture will get oxygen to their brains to help them think.

What to Say
Remember that the heart is a muscle. When it beats, it sends blood through our body. Some of that blood goes to our brain and helps us think more powerfully. If we slump or slouch, the blood has a harder time getting to our brain.

Why It's Important
Arteries carry oxygen-rich blood from the left side of the heart all over the body. Slouching can put a "kink" in the arteries alongside the neck, and the brain (especially the PFC) doesn't get a full supply of that oxygen-rich blood, making it harder to be mindful and focused.

the Optimistic™ classroom library

Mindful Movement II

What More Can We Learn About Mindful Movement?

Mindful movement begins with the awareness of our constantly changing physical sensations, as described in Lesson 8. We can build on this awareness by using movement challenges to help our brains focus and work more efficiently.

Why Revisit Mindful Movement?

In this second lesson on mindful movement, children continue to deepen their awareness of physical sensations they often overlook. From their Mindful Relaxing and Mindful Moving activity in the last lesson, children learned how to exercise vigorously to accelerate their heart rate and use breathing to calm their heart; they discovered that they could both mindfully observe and help control their physical responses. With this understanding, children are ready to try a set of physical challenges that require focus and concentration in order to maintain their balance. Participating in the balancing activity helps children deepen their brain-body connection and build self-regulation skills as they work to control their physical and emotional responses to stay steady.

In addition, children work on strengthening their decision-making abilities in this lesson. Working on our physical balance is shown to have positive effects on our brain's health, reinforcing higher-order thinking skills and emotional control.

What Can You Expect to Observe?

"My class loves taking movement breaks to help them refocus throughout the day. Once they've done mindful balancing, they want to try their own variations. I use cues like 'watch your personal space' and 'notice how close you are to your neighbors' to help them get a sense of how they are using the space around them. That awareness-building helps them to share the space around them."

—First-grade teacher

Linking to Brain Research

Emotional Balance:
Key to Efficient Executive Function

Executive function is mental management that takes the big picture into account. Executive function comprises many higher-order skills that depend upon the thinker's ability to reflect before reacting. Among these skills are evaluating information, organizing, focusing attention, prioritizing, planning, and problem solving. The control of executive function is guided by our prefrontal cortex, proportionally the largest of any primate. Executive function skills are affected by our emotional state in part because the neural networks for emotional response overlap with the neural networks for executive function. Thanks to the brain's neuroplasticity, both of these overlapping networks in the prefrontal cortex are strengthened when the brain is engaged in either an emotional response or an executive function.

Learners who can recognize and control their own emotional state become confident and successful, both socially and academically. Neuroscientist Adele Diamond notes that "activities that often get squeezed out of school curricula, such as the arts and physical exercise, are excellent for developing executive function skills [and] improving children's emotional state and social skills, and can be critical for academic success and for success later in life" (2009). Engaging in physical challenges, the arts, and mindful practices that enhance learning and reduce stress activate both emotional response and executive function networks simultaneously.

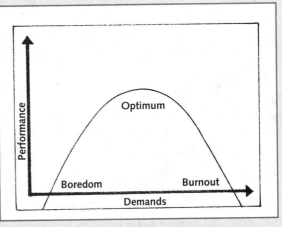

Some stress is necessary to normal functioning, but ever increasing amounts of stress produce diminishing returns on learning, achieving, socializing, and living.

Clarify for the Class

Mindful walking combines mindfulness with movement. Walk with your head floating like a balloon, paying attention to moving through the space in front of you and focusing on your breathing. Feel your breath coming in and going out fully. Encourage your mind not to wander by bringing other thoughts back to your breathing.

Discuss: Does moving around help you think sometimes?

Getting Ready

Make It Balanced
By using blocks to experiment with balance, children better understand the concept of balance in their own bodies.

GOALS

*   Children mindfully control their balance and describe the sensations they experience.
*   Children will connect mindful balancing to being well-balanced in life.

MATERIALS

*   set of building blocks
*   class set of small beanbags or any other object children can safely balance on their heads (e.g., soft plastic CD cases or notepads)

PREPARATION TIPS

*   Make space in the classroom for children to do exercises safely around their desks, or find a clear area such as the gym or an outdoor court.
*   For children with special physical needs, discuss appropriate adjustments for the balancing activities with the P.E. teacher, nurse, and parents, as needed.

CREATING THE OPTIMISTIC CLASSROOM

Brain-Inspired Instruction Taking brain breaks, described on page 86, can help balance high-intensity instruction with lower-intensity activities. Other ways to create a relaxed, brain-friendly classroom environment include the following:

*   singing
*   walking around the room and chatting with friends
*   listening to music
*   having a few pages of a classroom book read to them
*   sharing a joke

Steady, Now
Younger children just developing stability in their bodies may need help holding a balancing pose.

MINDUP Warm-Up

Building Balance Practice

Place one block on a stable surface, such as a desk or a table. Tell children that together you're going to stack the blocks to build the tallest tower you can. Carefully place a second block on top of the first one. Think aloud as you line up the sides of the blocks.

- *I want the blocks to stay steady. I don't want them to fall over, so I'll make sure the edges are even.*

Call on children, one by one, to add a block to the tower. When it looks as if the tower is about to collapse, add a block to throw it off balance, so no one child will feel responsible. Ask how your placement of the last block might have caused the tower to fall. Encourage children to model their ideas with the blocks; for example, placing one block on top of another without aligning the sides.

Repeat the activity.

- *Let's use what we learned to build another tower. We'll see if we can carefully balance the blocks on top of each other so they don't fall.*

Discuss: Which tower was taller? What is the best way to place the blocks on top of each other so they don't fall?

Leading the Lesson

Balancing Exercises

Engage	**Explore**

What to Do

Remind children that they've been practicing mindful behaviors, including mindful moving. Explain that today you're going to practice balance.

- We've been practicing mindful behaviors. We know how to breathe deeply to relax. We know how to pay attention to our body when we walk.

- Our body and brain work together to keep us balanced.

- Today, we're going to work on our balance.

Encourage children to share memories of when they were aware of their balance.

- My dog can't walk up the stairs very well, so I carry him. I move very mindfully up the stairs so I won't drop him.

- Tell me about a time when you moved carefully to keep your balance.

Model the first balance exercise for children. Stand still in an open space. Extend your arms. (Children should be able to do this without touching anyone.) Take a few deep breaths. Lift your right foot off the ground. Balance for 20–30 seconds. Let your foot touch down if you feel very unsteady. Ask children to pay close attention to the sensations they feel as they do the exercise.

- Plant your feet very firmly on the ground. Take deep, slow breaths to relax.

- Pick a spot in the room to focus on. This can help you balance.

- If you lose your balance, bring your foot down. Balance yourself and try again.

Have children do the exercise by lifting their left foot. For the second exercise, ask them to balance a beanbag on their head and lift one leg.

Why It's Important

Children may take their sense of balance for granted. The struggles of learning to stand up and walk as a toddler are long forgotten. Focusing on balancing exercises reinforces the importance of balance to children.

By concentrating on a focal point, children can engage their PFC. If their amygdala is shouting warnings about itchy toes and wobbly feet, children can redirect their focus and energy on standing upright and strong.

From the Research

Research shows that activities ... such as the arts and physical exercise, are excellent for developing executive function skills and can be critical for academic success and for success later in life. (Diamond, 2009)

Reflect

Talk about both exercises with children.

- When you first balanced on your leg, how did you feel?

- What did you stare at to keep your focus? How did that help you?

- What was the hardest part of balancing on one leg?

- Were you able to balance with the beanbag on your head?

- How did the beanbag change your balance?

Guide the discussion to make sure you've covered the key points from both mindful-balancing activities.

- When our bodies and brains work together, we can focus and think clearly.

- When we pay attention to the signals our body sends, our brain's ability to focus improves.

- Like all the other mindful activities, mindful movement and balancing helps our prefrontal cortex practice focusing.

As children become more adept at achieving and maintaining balance, they will have the confidence to try more challenges. They are developing their focus and awareness of (and trust in) the connection between their brain and their body.

MINDUP
In the Real World

Career Connection

Imagine walking on narrow beams of steel more than 1,000 feet in the air. If you're a high-rise ironworker, mindful movement—combining graceful agility with a keen sense of balance—not only enables you to do your job, but also helps guarantee your survival. When you're 100 flights up, overlooking a busy city street, one false step could mean a tumble to your death. While ironworkers take safety precautions such as ropes, harnesses, and safety nets, their best hope for survival is their own mindful movement—while being completely tuned in to all that's going on around them.

Discuss: If you're very skilled at keeping your balance, what other jobs might be a good fit for you? Think about people who might have to know how to stay steady while holding something, like a photographer or camera operator?

Once a Day

Try a simple balancing action, such as standing on one foot whenever you or the children are waiting (e.g., in line at the cafeteria, at dismissal). Balancing takes no preparation and keeps children focused and aware.

Connecting to the Curriculum

Mindful movement supports children's connection to their own learning process and to the content areas and literature.

Journal Writing

Encourage children to reflect on what they've learned about mindful movement and to record questions to explore at another time. They may also enjoy responding to these prompts:

- Imagine that you work in the circus. You have a job for which balance is very important. How would the ringmaster introduce you to the crowd? Draw a circus poster that shows you at work. Include the ringmaster. In a speech balloon, write what he or she would say.

- Write a story about a character who tries to balance something on top of his or her head—hats or eggs or a basketball! Illustrate your story.

- Many animals must be able to balance and control their bodies to find food or survive. Think of an animal that fits this description. Complete this sentence about the animal:

  A _____ must be able to balance because _____.

- **Pre-K & Kindergarten:** Have children draw a picture of a person or animal balancing on a surface; for example, a cat on a tree limb or a girl skating on ice.

PHYSICAL EDUCATION
On the Balance Beam

What to Do
Find a space where children will have room to walk—around the perimeter of the classroom, in the gym, or outside. Create a "balance beam" for them to walk along. You can make a 6-foot straight line out of masking tape or use a wooden 2"-by-4". Have children take turns walking heel to toe along the balance beam. For added difficulty, children can balance a beanbag on their heads.

What to Say
Have you watched gymnasts in action—maybe at a class or on television? They dance and tumble. They also work on a balance beam. A balance beam is a long narrow beam, or board. It's raised off the floor. A gymnast walks back and forth along its length and does other moves. Today, we're going to walk a balance beam on the floor. Walk heel to toe. Use your arms to help you balance.

Why It's Important
Walking heel to toe in a straight line produces a different sensation than does normal walking. Children must use their prefrontal cortex to help them focus and maintain their balance. Their arms and legs and bodies and brains must work together.

LANGUAGE ARTS
Spin and Balance

What to Do
Do this activity outside on a soft, flat surface. Ask children to stand still and describe how their bodies feel. Then tell them to start spinning until you signal them to stop. Allow 10–15 seconds for them to spin. Encourage children to talk about how their bodies feel after spinning and what they can do to regain their balance.

What to Say
Please stand quietly. How does your body feel? Can you feel your brain and your body working together to keep you in balance? First, I want you to start slowly spinning. When I give you the signal, I want you to stop. Ready? Spin. . . . Stop. How does your body feel now? Use mindful movement to help you regain your balance. Tell me how that helped.

Why It's Important
Children will be thrown off balance throughout their life, and they need to be prepared to re-balance their body. Mindful moving will keep them aware of their body in space and help them avoid injury.

MATH
Balancing on Shapes

What to Do
Have children experiment with balancing on different three-dimensional shapes: a balance ball, a cube, a rectangular bench, and so on. Begin by asking them to identify the shape of each object. Then ask them to take turns sitting on each object. Discuss which object was the easiest to balance on and which was the most difficult. Guide children to understand that shapes with flat faces are easiest to balance on.

What to Say
Look at these objects. Which three-dimensional shape does each one have? Which shape has six faces? Which shape has no faces? Now, please take turns sitting on each object. Which object was the easiest to sit on? Yes, it's easy to balance on a cube or a rectangle. It's hard to balance on the ball. Why? That's right. A face is a flat surface. It's easy to sit on. A ball is curved. It doesn't have a flat surface, so it can move out from under us.

Why It's Important
Children reinforce the neural pathways that help them identify shapes by physically touching them and understanding how the characteristics of each shape affect their balance.

SOCIAL-EMOTIONAL LEARNING
Run as One

What to Do
Have pairs of children work together to complete a three-legged race. Match children who are roughly the same height. As they stand side by side with their arms around each other's waist, tie their inside legs together with a scarf or strip of fabric. Make sure the material won't get in the way as children run. Set up a racecourse with a start and a finish line. Give pairs a chance to practice before racing.

What to Say
Today, we're going to have a three-legged race. Partners, stand beside each other. Place your arms around each other's waist. I'll tie your inside legs together. You'll race this way. Practice moving before the race begins. Think about how you can mindfully move together. Focus on helping each other and keeping your balance.

Why It's Important
This collaboration will expand children's experience with how their body moves. They'll have to work together to run as one and use their practice of mindful moving to help support each other.

Literature Link
Owl Moon

by Jane Yolen
(1987). New York: Scholastic

In this Caldecott Award book, a young girl and her father go owling one winter night. The girl must control her excitement, her voice, and her movements so she doesn't scare away the owl.

Children will enjoy giving the main character advice about how to use mindful behaviors to control her excitement, her voice, and her movements.

More Books to Share

Brown, Marc. (1999). *D.W. Flips*. Logan, IA: Perfection Learning.

Gerstein, Mordicai. (2003). *The Man Who Walked Between the Towers*. Brookfield, CT: Roaring Brook Press.

Nevius, Carol. (2004). *Karate Hour*. New York: Marshall Cavendish.

It's All About
Attitude

As students learn new ways to cultivate a positive mind-set, they prime their brain for learning and for building healthy relationships.

The findings of researchers in the field of psychology seem logical: cultivating happiness in our lives has myriad benefits emotionally, socially, and physically—we relate to others better, we treat ourselves well, and we are more likely to adopt healthy habits and avoid destructive behaviors.

But can happiness really help us get smarter? Yes! Cognitive studies have shown that learning that is connected with a happy or positive emotional experience causes the information to get stored in our long-term memories, while learning that takes place in conditions that cause stress and anxiety is stored only in short-term memory; it is not available for long-term use (Pawlak et al, 2003; Shadmehr & Holocomb, 1997).

That's a research-based incentive to bring more laughter and joy into our lessons. Helping students develop skills in relating better to others and making happy memories of what they learn are key goals of the three lessons in this unit.

Perspective Taking

What is Perspective Taking?

We live in a "small world" with as many different ways of seeing things as there are people. Perspective taking allows us to consider more than one way of understanding a behavior, event, or situation. This skill is particularly useful on a global scale as our ability to communicate and our need to share resources with other people and cultures expands.

Why Practice Perspective Taking?

On the most practical level, children who are able to accept that other classmates may behave or think differently than they do are much better equipped to tolerate and find ways to get along with peers. These children can talk out a problem and find a solution that is mutually agreeable.

Perspective taking, like the Core Practice and other mindful skills, simply takes practice to develop. As children routinely identify other perspectives, they learn to think with an "open mind"—to pause and consider other viewpoints mindfully.

This increasing ability to consider a situation in multiple ways has social benefits, such as reducing conflicts among children, facilitating group work, and cultivating an inclusive peer community. Perspective taking is an essential skill for problem solving in all subject areas, from understanding conflict in literature to finding strategies for problem solving in math and science.

What Can You Expect to Observe?

"I've found that asking children to think about the feelings of the characters we read about and to make a guess about why they're acting in a certain way gives them the practice and the language to consider why another child might have made a choice they disagree with."

—Kindergarten teacher

Linking to Brain Research

Opening the Mind to the Prefrontal Cortex

Perspective taking is the ability to see situations and events from the viewpoint of another person. When we mindfully practice perspective taking, we become more skilled at accurately interpreting the behavior of those around us. Mentally standing in someone else's shoes requires reflection, which can forestall an unthinking reaction. Repeatedly viewing issues or events through different lenses builds and strengthens the neural networks that enable us to reason before we take action. Paying attention to a situation in a calm, focused, mindful manner is a physiological workout for the brain, actually stimulating blood flow to it. Calm perspective taking directs incoming information on to the reflective, thinking prefrontal cortex instead of to the reflexive, reactive amygdala.

As students learn to consider alternate points of view, they can more effectively quell their own anxieties, exercise impulse control, and gauge their own behaviors and reactions in response to others. When differences of opinion are honored, and disagreement is respectful, students perceive the classroom as safe and risk-free. This unstressed state of mind allows their amygdala to "stand down" and puts the prefrontal cortex in control. A brain that operates primarily in the prefrontal cortex makes superior decisions, facilitating good choices for its owner.

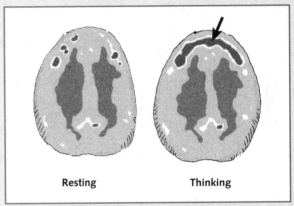

Resting   **Thinking**

These scans show where blood is flowing in the brain. Notice the increased blood flow in the prefrontal cortex area (arrow) of the thinking brain.

Clarify for the Class

Folding paper can help children understand how pathways of nerve cells are built through repeated practice, such as frequently identifying how others are feeling. Explain that, similar to moving information along a well-traveled path of connected nerve cells, refolding an already creased paper is faster and easier than folding a new sheet. Instruct children to fold a sheet of paper in half, and in half again to make fourths. Next ask them to unfold the paper until it's a flat sheet again, and then refold it.

Discuss: Was the paper easier to fold the second time? What are some things that are easier to do a second or third time? Do you think it's easier for your brain to think the same thing, or something new?

Getting Ready

What Was That Character Thinking? Wondering about the thoughts and actions of characters in the books you share with children encourages young readers to consider the perspective of others.

GOALS

- Children identify different perspectives of characters in a story.
- Children apply open-minded perspective taking to social situations in their own lives.

MATERIALS

- chart paper
- picture book of a fairy tale or fable (stories well suited to this lesson include "The Three Little Pigs," "The Tortoise and the Hare," "Goldilocks and the Three Bears," and "The Three Billy Goats Gruff")
- Character Feelings activity sheet (p. 156)

CREATING THE OPTIMISTIC CLASSROOM

Brain-Inspired Instruction Mindful perspective taking builds a strong support system in a classroom community that respects differences, enjoys collaboration, and honors cooperation. Positive experiences with participation and open-mindedness in class lead to even more positive experiences. Create powerful opportunities to explore others' feelings and behaviors as often as possible by acknowledging a child's feelings, even when his or her behavior is inappropriate. ("Of course you are excited about your birthday, but your excitement cannot distract us when we're working and learning.")

Let's Connect
Encouraging pair-share time
regularly encourages children
to listen to one another,
building a foundation for
perspective taking.

MINDUP Warm-Up

Perspective-Taking Practice
Guide children to identify emotions in themselves and others with this activity. Write the following sentence on chart paper: I am <u>happy</u>.

As you read the sentence, show children your happy face. Then write a sentence that expands on the first one, for example: I am <u>happy</u> when I teach you.

Keep your happy face on as you read this sentence. Then ask children to show you their happy face. Call on several children to tell what makes them happy. Remind them that their hippocampus, their memory saver, will help them think of memories.

Repeat the activity with other emotion words: *sad, angry, scared,* and *surprised.*

Pair children and let them take turns identifying an emotion on each other's face.

PRE-K CORNER: Draw a simple face showing the appropriate emotion beside each pair of sentences.

Discuss: What are some of the things that make us happy? Each of us is different. We have different memories and experiences. Seeing a spider might scare me, but it might not scare you. Why is it important to be able to look at someone's face and recognize how he or she is feeling?

Leading the Lesson

Out of Character

Engage

Explore

What to Do

Read aloud a picture book based on a fairy tale or fable (see Materials section for suggestions). Then review the story.

- Who is this story about?

- What is the first thing that Goldilocks did inside the bears' house?

- What did Goldilocks do next?

- After Goldilocks broke the chair, what did she do?

- What did the bears see when they came home?

- What happened when the bears found Goldilocks?

Discuss whether Goldilocks was behaving in a mindful way. Ask children to cite specific examples in the story that showed mindful or unmindful behavior. Remind them to avoid labeling the characters' behavior as "good" or "bad."

Display a copy of the Character Viewpoints activity sheet. With children's input, write the title of the fairy tale or fable and the main character on it. Then ask them to take the point of view of the character to delve more deeply into his or her thoughts and feelings.

- Imagine that you're Goldilocks.

- What were you thinking and feeling when you went into the house? When you ate the porridge? When you sat in the chairs? When you saw the beds? When you woke up and saw the bears?

Let children choose one of the events. Complete the activity sheet with their input. Now ask children to put themselves into the story. What would they have done in Goldilocks's place?

- You knock on the front door. No one answers. Will you go inside?

- Suppose you do go inside. Will you touch the bears' things?

- How would you feel when you woke up and saw the bears?

Why It's Important

Fairy tales and fables offer rich opportunities for studying mindful behavior and identifying and labeling emotions in others. Although the settings and situations are not realistic, children still empathize with the dilemmas the characters face. With guidance in perspective taking, they'll be able to broaden their view of story characters and real people.

Children step into the character's shoes to develop their understanding of his or her behavior. Then comparing that character's behavior to their own allows them to look at the story from another perspective.

Reflect

Encourage children to use what they know about mindful behavior to change an event in the story or to create a new ending for it.

- What happened when Goldilocks woke up and saw the bears? Which part of her brain took charge?

- What would have happened if Goldilocks's PFC had taken charge?

Allow time for pairs to act out the changed event or new ending to the story.

Key points that children are working toward understanding are:

- Different people may have different reactions to and different views or opinions about the same event.

- When we mindfully consider others' perspectives, we are less likely to make quick judgments and decisions, which can often be unfair.

MINDUP
In the Real World

Career Connection

Peace negotiators typically possess both an abundance of imagination and unique powers of persuasion that enable them to help those locked in conflict to transcend their own narrow views, take the perspective of the other, and bend toward a mutually acceptable solution. "Walk a mile in my shoes" is another way of saying "step outside of yourself and imagine what it feels like to be me."

Discuss: You are learning to be curious about how other people feel and think. How might you use those skills as a coach or a news reporter?

Once a Day

Choose a different child each day to focus on; observe closely; listen in on his or her conversations; talk one-on-one. Your close attention can help you better understand how the child approaches his or her work and relationships—invaluable information for building community and differentiating instruction.

Connecting to the Curriculum

Perspective taking supports children's connection to their own learning process and to the content areas and literature.

Journal Writing

Encourage children to reflect on what they've learned about perspective taking and to record questions to explore at another time. They may also enjoy responding to these prompts:

- Choose an emotion. Create a story mask for that emotion and draw it in your journal. Use colors and patterns to show how you feel when you experience the emotion.

- Write a story called "The Four Little Pigs." Imagine that you're the fourth pig. What is your house built of? Does the wolf succeed in blowing down your house? How does adding a character change the story?

- Think of a food that you like to eat. You share that food with a friend. Your friend doesn't like the taste. Describe what your friend's face looks like.

- **Pre-K & Kindergarten:** Share "Jack and Jill" with children. Ask them to pretend to be either Jack or Jill and continue the story. Have children draw a final scene. Scribe the text they create to go with their artwork in the Visual Journal.

LANGUAGE ARTS
My Side of the Story

What to Do
Turn the fairy story or fable you used in the lesson on its head. If you used "Goldilocks and the Three Bears," have children tell the story from the perspective of the three bears. You can put older children into groups of four—the three bears and Goldilocks—and ask them to write the revised story. Encourage younger children to draw the revised story. Set aside time for children to act out their revisions.

What to Say
We read "Goldilocks and the Three Bears." We tried to understand why Goldilocks did what she did and how she felt. Now let's think about the bears. Let's tell the story from their point of view, or perspective. They left their house. Where did they go? What did they do? What were they thinking and feeling when they got home? Someone was in their house! Write the story of The Three Bears and Goldilocks.

Why It's Important
In taking a different perspective on a familiar story, children must think more deeply about the characters and their motivations as they change the point of view of the story.

SOCIAL STUDIES
One World

What to Do
Bring in some travel magazines. Ask children to browse through them and choose a place that looks different from where they live. Encourage them to compare living in that place to living where they do. Talk about the similarities and differences between the places. Record children's responses on a chart under headings such as "food," "house," "clothes," and so on.

What to Say
We need food, water, and air. To protect ourselves, we live in houses and wear clothes. We play and work. Choose pictures of a place that looks different from where you live. Imagine living there. What would you eat? Where would you live? What would you wear? What would be different and what the same about living there?

Why It's Important
As humans, we all share the same basic needs—food, shelter, and so on. Our surroundings shape the form that these needs take. To empathize with those who seem to have different lives or values, begins with recognizing similarities and appreciating differences.

the **Optimistic** classroom™ journal

ART
A New View

What to Do
Pair children. Place a number cube or a letter block on a table and position partners on opposite sides of the object. Ask them to draw the object from their own perspective. Then have children compare their drawings and perspectives.

What to Say
Please sit down across from each other. I'm going to place an object in between you. Draw the object exactly as you see it. Look carefully and then draw. Now, sit together and compare your drawings. You have drawn the same object. Does the object look the same in both drawings? What looks the same? What looks different?

Why It's Important
Children use mindful seeing to observe the object, then further develop their perspective-taking skills by comparing their drawings and realizing that, although they drew the same object, each had a different perspective.

SOCIAL-EMOTIONAL LEARNING
Bilingual Tales

What to Do
Select a bilingual version of a fairy tale, such as "Caperucita Roja/Little Red Riding Hood." If you are not fluent in the second language of the text, ask someone who is to read it aloud. Then read aloud the English version. Have children share their thoughts and feelings as they tried to understand a text in a language they didn't know.

What to Say
If you grew up speaking English, then it seems natural that we speak English in class. That's not how someone feels who is learning English. Today, we're going to read a story you know—Little Red Riding Hood—in Spanish. As you listen and try to understand, pay attention to your thoughts and feelings.

Why It's Important
Children may not realize the obstacles that their classmates are confronting. Hearing a story in their native language will give ELLs an added boost, and all children will benefit from matching words in the two languages.

Literature Link
I Will Never Not Ever Eat A Tomato
by Lauren Child
(2000). New York: Scholastic.

Lola declares that "peas are too small and too green" and that "carrots are for rabbits." But her big brother Charlie knows just what to do to get her to sample everything on her plate! He playfully explains that what she thinks are carrots are really "orange twiglets from Jupiter." As the game continues, Lola discovers that this new perspective makes all of her food sound delicious!

Children will enjoy thinking about this new perspective of familiar food.

More Books to Share

Hamilton, Virginia. (2000). *The Girl Who Spun Gold*. New York: Blue Sky Press.

Myers, Walter Dean. (2000). *The Dragon Takes a Wife*. New York: Scholastic.

Wallner, John. (1987). *City Mouse-Country Mouse and Two More Tales from Aesop*. New York: Scholastic.

the Optimistic™ classroom library

Choosing Optimism

What is Optimism?

Optimism is a way of seeing life hopefully and having an expectation of success and well-being. It correlates strongly with good health and effective coping strategies. Optimism is a learned trait and if practiced, can become a way of thinking.

Why Practice Optimism?

Choosing to view life optimistically can increase our brain capacity; it relaxes our amygdala, creates chemical balance in our brains, and allows our prefrontal cortex to take charge. In this frame of mind, children learn that they can make much better choices than if they take a negative or pessimistic approach, which effectively shuts down their higher-level thinking.

Practicing optimism also makes it easier to learn—optimistic thinkers prime their brains to be ready to focus and make more room for new information to be absorbed and new ideas to stretch their wings. Socially, practicing optimism allows children to strengthen their perspective-taking skills and accept viewpoints different from their own, as well as connect with other people. In this lesson, children explore the benefits of optimism and see how pessimism can negatively affect their ability to think and learn, make friends, and solve common problems. With pessimism, a person gets bogged down and limits his or her ability to solve problems.

What Can You Expect to Observe?

"After this lesson, our class wanted to add to our class rules: 'Think optimistic thoughts.' Children instinctively get what this lesson and the activities about optimism and pessimism reinforce—being positive, being optimistic makes you feel better and clears your mind so you can think better. You might say our default mind-set is now optimism."
—Second-grade teacher

Linking to Brain Research

Optimism: A Learned Skill for Success

The research is clear—attitude matters! Children who are generally optimistic enjoy better physical health, have more success at school, flourish in relationships, and are more equipped to handle stress in their lives. Brain research has confirmed that optimism is more a learned trait than a genetic one. We can train our brain to have an optimistic perspective, thanks to neuroplasticity. This brain process forms new branching-off dendrites and more neuron-to-neuron connections during repeated experiences and practice. When children regularly use self-talk for positive thinking and to work through everyday frustrations, neuroplasticity creates and strengthens nerve cell (neuron) connections in their brains.

Optimism is easily identified in brain scans. Levels of dopamine and other brain neurotransmitters rise, cortisol levels remain steady, and the amygdala is open and forwarding information to the prefrontal cortex. An optimistic state of mind enables mindful response to stress and a downplaying of thoughts of failure, frustration, and hopelessness. Optimism breeds the expectation of success, which in turn makes it easier for the child to put forth the effort necessary for success.

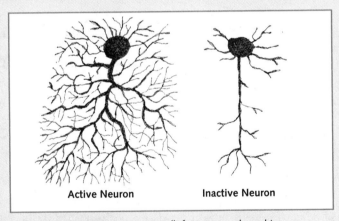

Active Neuron   **Inactive Neuron**

An active brain neuron, or nerve cell, forms many branching dendrites to make neural connections.

Clarify for the Class

Explain that thinking positively is something our brains can learn to do. By repeatedly having positive experiences and thinking positive thoughts, our brains learn to be optimistic, just as our bodies learn to do other tasks. Have children think of examples of positive self-talk, a strategy for boosting optimism.

Discuss: Can you zip a zipper or tie your shoes? How did you learn? Did it get easier with practice? How can we practice teaching our brain to think positively? What are some times during the day when we might need help to feel full of hope and anticipate good things happening? What are some reminders we can say to ourselves to boost good feelings and avoid feeling worried and discouraged?

Getting Ready

Sharing a Smile
Pairs treat one another to an optimistic expression.

GOALS
- Children will define two different mind-sets (optimism and pessimism) used to think about, react to, and approach a problem.
- Children will practice strategies that help them develop and maintain optimism in their own lives.

MATERIALS
- chart paper
- two white paper plates, two wooden craft sticks, glue
- (optional) Optimistic/Pessimistic Thoughts activity sheet (p. 157)

CREATING THE OPTIMISTIC CLASSROOM
Encouraging English Language Learners Your English language learners will experience frustration and discouragement in their journey to learn a new language and new concepts. Practicing optimistic thinking can boost their self-esteem and help them focus on learning. Be mindful of your own responses and how they can inadvertently derail a child's progress. Allow enough time for ELLs to process a question—at least a minute: "What animal did you draw?" If necessary, rephrase the question and model an answer: "This looks like a kangaroo. Is that right? Can you say, 'I drew a kangaroo'?"

My Optimistic Face
Trying on different expressions in
front of a mirror in the dramatic
play area can help children identify
their "optimistic" face.

MINDUP Warm-Up

Identifying Optimism/Pessimism

Act out an optimistic face and posture. Ask children to guess how you're feeling.
List their responses on the left side of a T-chart on chart paper, the chalkboard, or
the whiteboard. Spur the discussion by saying, "I feel so _____" and letting children
complete the sentence. Look for responses, such as *happy, cheerful, joyful*, and
hopeful. Ask children what clues they used to tell how you were feeling.

Repeat the activity. Act out a pessimistic face and posture. Look for responses, such
as *sad, worried, feeling blue, upset*, and *hopeless*. List them on the right side of the
T-chart.

Ask pairs to work together to suggest a label for each column and then have them
share their ideas with the class. Encourage older children and proficient writers to
copy the T-chart and add their labels.

Discuss: You were able to look at my face and my body to see how I was feeling.
How do you feel when you are around someone who is feeling happy and hopeful?
How do you feel when you are around someone who is feeling sad and hopeless?

PRE-K CORNER: Draw a happy face and an unhappy face to label each column.

Leading the Lesson

That's a Happy Face

Engage

What to Do

Create a happy face fan and a sad face fan out of paper plates and wooden craft sticks. Ask children to think about the warm-up activity as they look at the faces. Guide them to understand that optimists usually face a problem with the belief that success is possible with practice and focused work. Pessimists often become discouraged and frustrated when facing a problem.

- Which face shows someone who is thinking happy thoughts? This person feels hopeful about solving a problem. This person practices optimistic thinking.

- Which face shows someone who is thinking unhappy thoughts? Problems discourage this person. This person is a pessimistic thinker.

- We can choose to be optimistic thinkers.

Read the following statements aloud (or create your own examples). Have children raise their hand if the statement shows optimistic thinking.

"It's raining! We can't have our picnic."
"It's raining! We can have our picnic inside."

Why It's Important

Note that the terms *optimistic thinking* and *pessimistic thinking* are less judgmental than *optimist* and *pessimist*. Children who recognize both types of thinking can learn to experience optimism as a daily practice.

Explore

Give children a scenario they can relate to and ask them to see it from an optimistic and a pessimistic perspective. For example, have children imagine that the school principal walks by, frowning. They say "hello," but the principal keeps walking without responding.

- You're an optimistic thinker. What do you think?

- You're a pessimistic thinker. What do you think?

PRE-K CORNER: Offer this scenario to younger children who may not have experience with a principal: You are building a tower out of blocks. You're working really hard. A classmate bumps the tower, and it falls over.

Scribe an answer on a display copy of the Optimistic/Pessimistic Thoughts activity sheet. Then talk about the role of the brain in optimistic thinking.

- What happens to the brain of optimistic thinkers? The amygdala is calm. It sends information to the prefrontal cortex. That helps us think more clearly.

The PFC receives more and clearer information and feelings from a calm amygdala and, therefore, works much better when children look at the bright side of things and believe that problems can be solved. Behavioral scientists have found that optimistic thinkers are actually happier and healthier and do better in school and life than pessimistic thinkers.

From the Research
Mindfulness has been found to be related to well-being, including optimism, positive affect, self-regulation, and lower rates of depression and anxiety.
(Brown & Ryan, 2003)

Reflect

Have children examine their own perspective. Ask partners to talk about how they would feel in the scenario described in the Explore section. Then guide children in generating a list of strategies they can use to adopt an optimistic perspective so their brain can stay healthy and work better.

- Think about the scene we imagined with the principal.

- Were you able to see both points of view?

- How would you have felt—like an optimistic thinker or a pessimistic thinker?

- Think of all the mindful behaviors we've learned. How can we practice to be more optimistic thinkers?

Record children's ideas on a "Think Happy!" class list that you can post in the room. Ideas might include looking at a problem from another perspective, replacing a negative thought about something with a positive one, reminding ourselves that a worry is a feeling that can pass, doing a mindful breathing or sensing exercise, playing a game, singing a song, or sharing a joke.

This reflection should guide children to conclude:
- Optimistic thinkers are happier, healthier, and more successful people.

- Optimistic thinking helps us solve problems.

- We can choose to be optimistic and practice optimism so it becomes a mind-set.

MINDUP In the Real World

Career Connection

A worker in a nursery spends his or her time tending seedlings, waiting for plants to sprout, keeping plants well watered and free from pests, and making sure that the growing season is a healthy, flowery one! Children may never have considered that a gardener could benefit from having an optimistic attitude. Remind them that anyone who depends on the weather and the cycle of seasons will face continual problems and unexpected circumstances. In a job like that, a positive attitude is as important as a spring rain!

Discuss: How could optimism help you if there were parts of your job that might change, like the weather? Think about farming or sailing.

Once a Day

Have children think of one thing they learned or enjoyed in class and tell it to you as they leave for the day. This helps you assess their accomplishments and highlights for them how they've benefitted from learning.

Connecting to the Curriculum

Learning about optimism supports children's connection to their own learning process and to the content areas and literature.

Journal Writing

Encourage children to reflect on what they've learned about choosing optimism and to record questions to explore at another time. They may also enjoy responding to these prompts:

- What is a problem you have solved recently? Write about the process of solving it, and how a positive, focused attitude helped you do so.

- Create a "Turn Your Frown Upside Down" page in your journal. Brainstorm ways to turn your frown upside down into a smile.

- Draw a picture of your brain thinking happy, or optimistic, thoughts. Add a caption to your drawing.

- **Pre-K & Kindergarten:** Generate a list of happy thoughts with children. Write down their ideas on strips of paper and put them in a bowl. Select one happy thought to share each day. Record that thought in each child's journal. Have children illustrate it.

the **Optimistic** classroom™ journal

MATH
That's Not a Problem

What to Do
Assign a math problem to half the class. The other half of the class will be optimistic-thinking coaches. Pair a problem solver and a coach. Review the importance of optimistic thinking in problem solving. Ask problem solvers to pay close attention to their thoughts and feelings as they work to solve the problem. Encourage them to think aloud so their coaches will know when to step in with some optimistic-thinking tips.

What to Say
Optimistic thinking helps us solve problems. We let the amygdala pass on information to the PFC, and we let the hippocampus remind us what we already know. I'm going to divide the class into Problem Solvers and Optimistic-Thinking Coaches. Problem Solvers will solve a math problem. Problem Solvers, think aloud as you work, so your coach can help you stay optimistic. Then you'll switch roles.

Why It's Important
Pessimistic thinking can derail a child's confidence in his or her ability to solve math problems. Switching roles allows children to benefit from the brain chemistry changes brought on by optimistic thinking, and to experience problem solving from another perspective.

SOCIAL STUDIES
Together, We Can Do It

What to Do
Explain to children what a "can-do" attitude is. Then talk about an issue at school or in the community that's of interest to your children, for example, updating the school's playground equipment. Challenge them to come up with a plan for participating. Ask them how an optimistic, "can-do" attitude might help them with their plan.

What to Say
A person who has a "can-do" attitude is an optimistic thinker. He or she says, "I can do that!" instead of "I can't do that!" Our school needs some "can-do" thinkers. Our playground is getting rundown. Let's work together to make a plan to fix it up.

Why It's Important
Children learn that they can have a positive impact on their community. When people with disparate perspectives work together, optimistic thinking is crucial for consensus and to accomplish common goals.

LANGUAGE ARTS/MUSIC
Happy Tunes

What to Do
During the course of a day, play a variety of upbeat songs, such as "If You're Happy and You Know It," or "The More We Get Together." After playing a song, ask children how the song made them feel. After a review of the songs, challenge children to write their own happy tunes. Record the songs on a class DVD and display the lyrics in a songbook.

What to Say
Today, we listened to some happy tunes. What was your favorite song? How did it make you feel? Did it help you think positive thoughts? Did you hum the song to yourself or whisper the words to help you relax and think more clearly? All these songs gave me a great idea for writing my own happy tune. Let's all write our own happy tune.

Why It's Important
Singing a song is one strategy children can use to bolster their optimism. In writing their own songs, children "own the words"; they build vocabulary, fluency, expressiveness—and tap into their own musicality.

SOCIAL-EMOTIONAL LEARNING
A Pessimistic Puppet

What to Do
Give each child a finger puppet to represent the voice inside their heads that says, "You can't do this!" Have children think of a hard problem they've faced and create an optimistic thinking/pessimistic thinking dialogue between themselves and their puppet. Older children and proficient writers can complete the Optimistic/Pessimistic Thoughts activity sheet.

What to Say
Pretend that your puppet is you—as a pessimistic thinker. Now think of a problem you've faced. Try to talk your puppet into becoming an optimistic thinker. Let me show you: Yesterday, I went to a drawing class. Me: I'd like to learn to draw better. Puppet: Everyone will laugh at you. Me: They're probably nervous, too.

Why It's Important
Pessimistic thinking can become automatic and seem to be our true voice. Role playing can help children take note of their own pessimistic thinking and help them channel their energy into optimistic thinking.

Literature Link
If You're Happy and You Know It
by James Warhola
(2007). New York: Scholastic.

The popular song goes wild in this "Jungle Edition"! A brother and sister transform a city playground when they imagine the jungle gym animals springing to life. As the kids leap into action to roar with a lion or laugh like a hyena, they make their own fun. Discuss how the words and actions in the song might make anyone feel happier and more optimistic.

More Books to Share
Frame, Jeron Ashford. (2003). *Yesterday I Had the Blues*. Berkley, CA: Tricycle Press.

Stevenson, James. (1999). *Don't Make Me Laugh*. New York: Farrar, Straus and Giroux.

Watt, Melanie. (2008). *Scaredy Squirrel*. New York: Scholastic.

the **Optimistic** classroom™ library

Appreciating Happy Experiences

What Does It Mean to Appreciate Happy Experiences?

We can make ourselves laugh over the memory of a hilarious situation shared with friends or flood ourselves with a feeling of warmth by recalling the hug of a beloved grandparent. To remember a happy experience fully and mindfully is to appreciate it and reap the physical, emotional, and cognitive benefits.

Why Appreciate Happy Experiences?

Remembering a happy memory releases the "feel-good" chemicals in our brain that flooded it at the time of the actual experience. We can practice mindfully recalling favorite memories as a strategy to achieve a variety of goals, including

• cultivating optimism
• alleviating negativity (e.g., boredom, worry)
• priming our brain for learning new material
• generating ideas from past experiences
• boosting our physical health

Children can learn to appreciate happy memories to help overcome specific negative feelings, such as sadness or insecurity. You can also integrate the concept into your teaching by creating learning experiences that are engaging and involve positive interactions and laughter, when possible. Those memories will be prioritized and easy for children to recall and build background from.

What Can You Expect to Observe?

"Some of my students don't have many happy memories to build on outside of school. In our classroom, one of my goals is to provide as many playful and fun moments around learning together as I can—these are shared experiences we can return to and build on. They make us resilient during difficult or sad times."

—First-grade teacher

Linking to Brain Research

Happy Memories Support a Can-Do Attitude

Recall from lessons 6 and 7 the critical role of the neurotransmitter most associated with pleasure, attention, reward, motivation, and perseverance—dopamine. Higher levels of dopamine in our brain result in feelings of hope, tolerance, motivation, and a can-do attitude—optimism. Dopamine release is triggered when we engage in pleasurable experiences like play-filled activities, laughing, physical exercise, kind gestures, and positive social interactions.

Brain scans show that dopamine is released not only when we engage directly in pleasurable experiences, but also when we reflect on and remember these salient moments. In fact, remembering a positive experience can trigger dopamine release as powerfully as the real thing. By repeatedly referencing past successes, we build confidence and are more able to rebuff the "I can't" voice in our head. Happy memories can become a tool to prime the brain for new social, academic, and physical challenges.

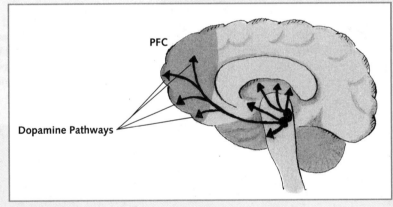

A major pathway of dopamine leads to the prefrontal cortex.

Clarify for the Class

Remembering "I did" is a great way to fight off "I can't"! Explain that when you feel the frustration and hopelessness of not being able to do something, bringing up a memory of something you did accomplish can help. Have children think of an activity he or she would like to be able to do, but feel he or she can't. For example: read a long book or learn to ride a bike. Then ask them to remember something related to their selected activities that they have done. For example, "read a short book," or "watched my big sister ride a bike." Challenge children to imagine themselves in the memory reading the book or observing the bike rider.

Discuss: Do you feel differently about your "I can't" after remembering something you had accomplished or experienced? How? Does it feel more possible now?

Getting Ready

Modeling From the Heart
A principal shares a happy
memory about this group
of kindergarteners.

GOALS
- Children visualize and describe their thoughts, feelings, and physical sensations during a pleasurable experience.
- Children use recalling a pleasurable experience as a way to build optimism.

MATERIALS
- chart paper

CREATING THE OPTIMISTIC CLASSROOM
Brain-Inspired Instruction Sharing your own happy memories gives children a great model and invites them to make a closer connection to you. In addition to telling children about childhood experiences and more contemporary experiences with your family, set aside time each day to celebrate a classroom event that pleased you the day before. For example, you might praise a child for picking up a piece of paper from the floor or for helping a friend, or the whole class for specific instances of mindful behavior. Children will see that you observe and honor their efforts.

"My Happy Memory"
Children use writing time to record and share happy memories, which will be collected to create a class book.

MINDUP Warm-Up

Memory-Sharing Practice

Share a happy memory about your class that makes you smile as you share it with children. For example, you might reveal a special moment from the first day of school, when you met them. Be as specific and descriptive as possible to help children remember their own memories from that day, too. If you took any photos on that day, share them to help trigger memories.

Then ask children to share their own memories. List those memories on chart paper. As you review the list, encourage children to smile and laugh as they think back. Let your face and body show your own honest response to each memory.

Discuss: Which memory made you smile most broadly? Which memory made you laugh? Did someone remember something that you had forgotten? Do you think your hippocampus has stored that happy memory now?

Leading the Lesson

My Happy Memory Movie

Engage

Explore

What to Do

Review the warm-up and remembering happy times as a way to practice optimistic thinking.

- Remembering our happy memories helps us practice optimistic thinking.

- Today, we're going to learn to remember as mindfully as we can.

Select a positive event that has occurred in your classroom, one that children are likely to remember, too. Model how to draw out and appreciate the memory. Narrate it aloud and let your expression show how happy the memory makes you feel.

- I'm going to show you how I think of a happy memory.

- I'm going to focus on where I was, who was with me, what was happening, and how I felt.

- I'll shut my eyes. I'll try to see the memory in my mind, like a movie.

Review how you focused on your memory and shared it with them. Emphasize that the memory was so clear that it felt as if you were watching a home movie.

Ask children to select their favorite memory from the list they created in the warm-up activity or choose another memory that made them especially happy, such as a playing with a friend, mastering a skill, or receiving a pleasant surprise.

Offer cues to help children fully visualize their memory. Begin and end the visualization with the sound of a bell, soft claps, or any other sound you've been using with your mindful practice.

- Bring all your attention to your happy memory.

- Look around you. Look at the people. Look at the place. Focus on the things that are making you happy.

- Picture how your happy memory ends.

- What are you thinking? How is your body feeling?

Why It's Important

Taking time to model how to recall a memory will help children understand that they must slow down and really notice the details that make the memory more complete and special. The mindful sensing activities that children have been practicing will come into play here, too, as they recreate the memory. Note: It's a good idea to practice telling your memory aloud before you present it to children.

Providing plenty of structure and quiet space for children to recall their memories will allow their amygdala to relax, their prefrontal cortex to receive and process all the input it's gathering, and their hippocampus to release the stored memory.

Reflect

Allow children a few moments to refocus their awareness on the classroom. Then guide them to share their experiences.

- As you enjoyed your memory, how did your brain feel? How did your body feel?

- How do you feel now?

Tell children that their brain can help change how their body and mind feel. Recalling happy memories is one way to do that.

Point out that while nobody is happy all the time, we can use happy memories as a tool to feel better, enjoy special times with friends and family, and build optimistic-thinking skills. Ask children to be very aware of happy moments that arise over the next few days. Remind them to "make a movie in their mind" to appreciate and revisit those happy feelings.

The experience of being flooded by warm emotions from the memory they chose proves to children that they can control their thoughts and feelings, even if they can't always control what happens around them. It also shows how quickly feelings can change. A simple mindful practice can quickly improve their mood.

MINDUP In the Real World

Career Connection

Pleasure may begin with our ability to notice and relish details—appreciation for a tasty soup, enjoyment of a shared song, and deep satisfaction from a handmade gift. One of the joys of being around young children is their natural ability to appreciate the smallest details of an experience. A prekindergarten teacher will often witness a sense of wonder and delight—splashing in a rain puddle, watching a butterfly, or playing with shadows on a wall—as she or he sees the world through the eyes of young children. Spending time with young children forces us to slow down and pay attention to the small details that are ours to savor, too.

Discuss: How do you notice people taking time during the day, especially when they are working, to enjoy themselves?

Once a Day

As you teach, think of creating a happy memory, whether you incorporate humor, a song, a game, or some other kind of positive group interaction. These memories will become a platform for new instruction.

Connecting to the Curriculum

Appreciating happy experiences supports children's connection to their own learning process and to the content areas and literature.

Journal Writing

Encourage children to reflect on what they've learned about appreciating happy experiences and to record questions to explore at another time. They may also enjoy responding to these prompts:

- Write a happy hint in your journal. Describe what to do when you feel a little blue and want to cheer yourself up.

- Think of a happy memory. How does your body feel? How does your face change? Write down what happens.

- What things make you laugh? Write down one or two and/or draw them.

- Create a happy poem. Start each line with a letter in the word *HAPPY*:

  H_____
  A _____
  P _____
  P _____
  Y _____

- **Pre-K & Kindergarten:** Ask parents or caretakers to send a photo of their child enjoying a happy time with family or friends. Have the child tell about that happy memory. Dictate the story in his or her journal.

SOCIAL STUDIES
Time Capsule

What to Do
Tell children that you want to collect some of their memories in a time capsule. Ask them to write about and/or draw a picture of a happy school memory and date it. Store their memories in a container. At the end of the year, open the container and revisit the memories. If possible, have children add memories over the course of the year. Maintain the time capsule for as long as possible so children will have a continuous record of their memories.

What to Say
We're going to make a time capsule. A time capsule contains information that is kept for a long time. When people open it in the future, they learn about life in an earlier time. Think back to one of your happiest school memories. Describe it in words and/or pictures. I'll store your memories in this container, and we'll open our time capsule at the end of the year.

Why It's Important
Contributing to a time capsule gives children a better sense of the past, present, and future and their own role in history. Their memories are important because they convey the sense of what their lives were like.

LANGUAGE
A Happy Spot

What to Do
Direct children in a video presentation about the importance of happiness. Review the impact of happiness on our health and how it affects our brain. For an opening title, have children create a "Be Happy!" poster that lists the benefits. Then ask each child to share a happy tip from his or her journal on camera.

What to Say
Today, we're going to create a short "Be Happy!" video. We know that optimistic thinking helps us feel good about ourselves and learn new things. We can become better optimistic thinkers by enjoying our happy experiences and remembering them later on. Our brain works better. Our amygdala passes on information to our PFC. Our hippocampus stores that information.

Why It's Important
Participating in this activity allows children to become the teachers, to spread the word about the benefits of appreciating and remembering happy experiences. Relaying the message to an audience underscores its importance.

the Optimistic™ classroom journal

ART
Happy Faces/Happy Bodies

What to Do

Create a class yearbook. Devote a page to each child. Snap a photo of each child's face as he or she thinks of a happy memory and as the child expresses happiness through movement. Finally, let each child complete the following statement for his or her page: _____ makes me happy.

What to Say

We're going to make a Happy Book for our classroom. Each of you will have your own page. Think of a happy memory, and I'll take a picture of your face. Show me how you move when you're happy, and I'll take a picture of your body. What makes you happy? Complete this sentence for your page: _____ makes me happy. You can also draw a picture of something that makes you happy.

Why It's Important

Happiness can be infectious. On down days, a child can look at his or her page in the Happy Book to get a lift. The memory of creating the page or mimicking the smile and movement in the photo can help brighten the day.

SOCIAL-EMOTIONAL LEARNING
A Shared Memory

What to Do

Explain the importance of sharing happy memories. For instance, someone may not realize that they have had a powerful, positive effect on us. That person's perspective of an event may be different from our own. Sharing a happy memory with someone can make that person happy, too, and a new memory is formed.

What to Say

Yesterday, a friend called me. She said she enjoyed seeing me at the farmer's market on Saturday. I've been really busy this week. I completely forgot about seeing her. But then I remembered what a good time we had. I just started smiling. It made feel really happy that she called. Now, you think about someone who's made you happy and let them know how you feel.

Why It's Important

Children learn to value other people and to express their appreciation. They become more mindful of how their own behavior can affect other people's lives.

Literature Link
Pablo's Tree

by Nancy Carlson
(1996). New York: Scholastic.

Abuelito had planted the tree when Pablo was a tiny baby. For each birthday since, his grandfather surprises the little boy by festooning the tree with a different type of decoration. As the story unfolds, readers get to share Pablo's happy memories of past birthdays and other special times he's experienced with Abuelito.

Connect to a discussion of family traditions and how some of our happiest times are those shared with family and friends.

More Books to Share

Henkes, Kevin. (2007). *A Good Day.* New York: Greenwillow.

McCloud, Carol. (2006). *Have You Filled a Bucket Today?* Northville, MI: Ferne Press.

Tamar, Erika. (1996). *The Garden of Happiness.* New York: Harcourt.

Taking Action
Mindfully

Learning to express gratitude and perform acts of kindness helps children build the awareness, cognitive skills, compassion, and confidence to contribute in a meaningful way to the classroom and the world.

Children gain an appreciation for special people and things in their lives and discover the social, emotional, and cognitive benefits of showing gratitude.

As children perform small acts of kindness for friends, classmates, teachers, and family, they learn how these positive actions can increase their optimism and brain power.

Children collaboratively plan and perform a group act of kindness and reflect on the way combined efforts can make an important difference in the world and connect them to their peers and the larger community.

"When you give yourself, you receive more than you give." The lessons in this unit give credence to Saint-Exupéry's famous quote. Certainly, there are obvious benefits for the recipients of kind actions children will do in these lessons—from helping lift a classmate's spirits to raising funds for victims of a natural disaster on the other side of the world. Yet participating mindfully in positive social actions can affect children's social, emotional, and cognitive growth in transformational ways.

By expressing gratitude and performing acts of kindness, children develop a stronger understanding of the feelings of other people and a concern for the well-being of others. Research shows that actions that engender feelings of empathy and compassion have a number of positive benefits, such as boosting the production of the feel-good neurotransmitter dopamine, increasing the likelihood that children will continue to act on their social concerns, and improving their capacity to take care of themselves.

Expressing Gratitude

What Is Gratitude?

Gratitude is a feeling of thankfulness and joy we feel in response to something we've received, whether the gift is tangible, such as a book we look forward to reading, or intangible, such as a smile of encouragement from a loved one or a breathtaking view of a landscape.

Why Practice Expressing Gratitude?

Simply focusing for a minute on the experiences in our lives we're grateful for shifts our thinking to a calmer, more content perspective, which can immediately uplift and comfort us. When we make the expression of gratitude a regular practice—whether we make a daily written list or a mental tally of things we're grateful for as we start or end each day—we train our brain to shift to a positive mind-set more efficiently and maintain a healthier, more optimistic perspective.

This lesson gives children the opportunity to identify and share with peers expressions of gratitude for people, events, and things in their lives. This sharing forges stronger connections and trust among peers. The mindful listening required in the lesson also cultivates children's empathy, laying the foundation for planning and performing acts of kindness over the course of the final two lessons.

What Can You Expect to Observe?

"At first, children were eager to share material things that they were grateful for, like games and toys. With practice, they now enjoy sharing the things that make them feel deeply thankful—a happy memory of playing with a friend, getting a tip on tying a shoe, having a tasty lunch."

—Kindergarten teacher

Linking to Brain Research

The Many Gifts of Gratitude

Gratitude has powerful physiological effects on the brain—and body. Researchers have found that when we think about someone or something we truly appreciate, our bodies calm themselves. The feelings that come with gratitude trigger the calming branch of the autonomic nervous system, the parasympathetic system. The sympathetic system is the "fight, flight, or freeze" responder during emergencies, stress, and intense activity. The counter-acting parasympathetic system is all about "rest and digest." It slows the heartbeat, shunts blood from the muscles to the organs, and contracts the pupils of the eyes. Feeling appreciative also produces a more even heart rhythm, which may reduce the risk of heart attacks and relieve hypertension.

Feeling thankful and appreciative also affects levels of brain neurotransmitters, including releasing dopamine toward the prefrontal cortex where reasoning and logic occur. Dopamine not only fosters contentment, it is also the main player in the brain's reward and motivation system. Experiments have shown that those who keep gratitude journals or lists feel more optimistic and make more progress toward their goals. And young people who do daily self-guided exercises in gratitude have higher levels of alertness, enthusiasm, determination, attentiveness, and energy. (McCullough et al., 2001) Children who practice grateful thinking not only have a more positive attitude toward school, their brains are more ready to learn.

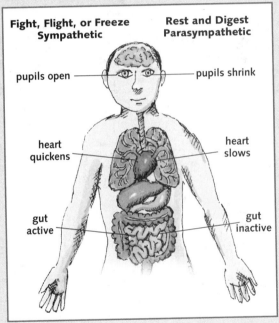

Fight, Flight, or Freeze Sympathetic   **Rest and Digest Parasympathetic**

pupils open — pupils shrink

heart quickens — heart slows

gut active — gut inactive

The autonomic nervous system has two parts: sympathetic and parasympathetic.

Clarify for the Class

Ask children to think about what their bodies are doing right now. Explain that many of our body functions work automatically, including breathing, digesting food, and pumping blood. We don't think about them—they just happen automatically. These kinds of functions are controlled by the autonomic nervous system. Draw a T-chart and label the left column "STRESSED" and the right "CALM." Ask children to describe what happens to their bodies during each state. When finished, explain that feeling gratitude helps calm the body and readies the brain to learn.

Discuss: What are some grateful thoughts that might calm your body? If you repeat them to yourself, do you feel different? How so?

Getting Ready

Gratitude, Naturally
Using mindfulness to carefully observe change in plants and other living things is one way to cultivate gratitude.

GOALS
- Children learn the meaning of gratitude and the importance of expressing gratitude.
- Children identify things in their life for which they are grateful.

MATERIALS
- chart paper
- construction paper for bulletin board tree (brown, green, yellow, red, and orange)

CREATING THE OPTIMISTIC CLASSROOM
Supporting English Language Learners While group discussions about gratitude are valuable for building active listening skills, not all children will feel comfortable sharing in such a setting. Gratitude journals, introduced in this lesson, offer a safe mode of expression for those children. English language learners, too, may prefer writing or drawing over speaking. Also encourage ELLs to act out situations that shows gratitude being shown. Express vocabulary that corresponds to their gestures and movements.

"Thank You!"
Children enjoy practicing gratitude by thanking their peers and teachers regularly with different gestures.

MINDUP Warm-Up

Remembering "Thank You's" Practice

Update children on your own progress with replaying memories to savor happiness. Share a memory where you expressed gratitude to someone; for example: "Yesterday, I lost a book. Mrs. Garza found it in the cafeteria and returned it to me. I felt happy to have the book back, and I was so grateful to Mrs. Garza for taking the time to return it."

Have children take a few deep breaths and then remember a time recently when they said "thank you" to someone. Then ask them to draw a picture of the memory. Call on a few volunteers to share their memory movies. What were they thankful for? Who did they thank?

On chart paper, list their responses under the heading "Thank you for...", such as "finding my book," "playing tag," "sharing your banana," and so on. After each response, ask if anyone has a similar memory: "Who thanked someone for playing?"

Discuss: Look at our list. When did we thank someone? What are some other ways that we can feel and show how thankful we are?

Leading the Lesson

Growing a Gratitude Tree

Engage

Explore

What to Do

Have children sit on the floor in a circle around you. Introduce and define the word *gratitude*: Gratitude is a feeling and a way of thinking that expresses our thanks. Give an example by sharing things you are grateful for, such as being healthy, learning new things every day in the classroom, and enjoying time with your family and friends. Build on expressions that children may be more familiar with, including "being grateful" or "being thankful."

- Here is our "Thank your for . . ." list from our warm-up activity. We are all grateful for many things in our lives.

- Today we're going to create a gratitude tree. You can see the tree's trunk on the bulletin board. The branches are empty. We're going to put leaves on the branches and make the tree grow.

Ask children to think of two people to whom they are grateful. Then show them how to draw and cut out two construction-paper leaves, or use a leaf template. Tell children to write a person's name on each leaf. As they attach each leaf to a branch of the gratitude tree, encourage children to share why they are grateful for that person. Remind the other children to listen mindfully.

PRE-K CORNER: Cut out the leaves for younger children and let them dictate the name for you to write on each leaf. Make the leaves large enough for children to add a drawing of the person.

- Think about two people you are grateful to. Take time to play memory movies about them in your mind.

- Write each person's name on a leaf. Place the leaf on the gratitude tree.

- Tell us why you are grateful to each person.

Keep a container or an envelope full of leaves near the bulletin board so children can continue to add leaves to the tree to make it grow.

Why It's Important

Cognitive research suggests that when we focus on the things we are grateful for, our happiness increases. Making a habit of expressing our gratitude helps us be mindful and leads us to a greater appreciation of other people and the larger world around us. Gratitude practice is a helpful tool to integrate into the school day.

Children may tend to remember happy memories of sweet snacks or toys. Focusing on expressing gratitude to a person helps children realize that happiness is not dependent on ownership and wealth. The generosity in another's person's action, or their own actions, are deeply satisfying.

Reflect

After a few days, review the additions to the gratitude tree. (You may want to color code the leaves so you can recognize the "new growth.")

- Look at how fast our tree is growing! It's getting so many leaves!

- How did you feel as you made a leaf and then put it on the tree?

- How do you feel now when you see your leaves?

Continue to review and celebrate the growth of the gratitude tree on a weekly basis.

When you build on children's responses to helping the gratitude tree grow, you help them recognize the positive effects that gratitude practices can have, such as improving our mood, helping us think more clearly, connecting us with the people we're grateful to, connecting us with others who are expressing gratitude, and giving us a sense of well-being or happiness.

MINDUP
In the Real World

Career Connection

Feeling grateful enables people in any circumstance to relax and experience a sense of peace and happiness. That's especially important when the type of task a person is doing is stressful, such as working late to meet a deadline, or tiring, such as spending many hours standing or sitting. One way to generate feelings of gratitude and find ways to do the work at hand even better is to seek feedback from coworkers and supervisors. When we receive genuine, constructive criticism from people whose goal is to help us do our job better, we discover new ways to do tasks or solve problems—and that is something to be grateful for!

Discuss: Think of a job or task you do often at school, such as reading announcements. How do other people help you do your job well? How do you show gratitude to them for their help?

Once a Day

Seek feedback from a colleague on the way you explain a concept, lead a routine, or implement a strategy. Consider how the perceptions and ideas of others can plant the seeds of growth.

Connecting to the Curriculum

Expressing gratitude supports children's connection to their own learning process and to the content areas and literature.

Journal Writing

Encourage children to reflect on what they've learned about expressing gratitude and to record questions to explore at another time. They may also enjoy responding to these prompts:

- Show your gratitude! Draw and decorate a medal or a ribbon to show who or what you're grateful for.

- G-R-A-T-I-T-U-D-E. Look at each letter in the word. What are you grateful for that starts with each letter? *G* is for games. Are you thankful for games?

- Write a message for the inside of a thank-you card.

- **Pre-K & Kindergarten:** Ask children to retell a fairy tale or favorite story with the emphasis placed on gratitude. For instance, how would the story of Cinderella change if the stepsisters showed their gratitude for Cinderella's hard work?

MATH
Sharing Parts of a Whole

What to Do
Reinforce the concept of sharing by having children work with fractions. Cut circles and squares out of construction paper to represent small pizzas and sandwiches. Let children decorate the shapes to look like food. Give each child a shape and ask them to decide the best way to share it with a friend.

What to Say
Pretend that these shapes are food. Each circle is one small pizza. Each square is one sandwich. Choose a shape and decorate to look like food. Now imagine this: You are about to sit down and eat your pizza or sandwich. A friend comes over. He or she looks very hungry. Divide your food into two equal pieces. Share it with your friend.

Why It's Important
Children create parts of a whole. They may fold their shapes in half to try to be as precise and fair as possible or use a pencil to divide the shape in half. This activity can be extended to work with other fractions, such as fourths and eighths. Older children can work in small groups of three or more to decide how to share.

SOCIAL STUDIES
Thanks! *Merci!* *¡Gracias!*

What to Do
On index cards or sticky notes, write down the word for "thank you" in several languages. Repeat each word several times and place the word card or note on the appropriate location on a world map or globe. Then ask children to select a "thank you" from the map or globe. Encourage them to use the word to express their gratitude.

What to Say
Everyone in the world feels and shows gratitude to others. Here we usually say "thank you." I'll put that word on the United States on the map. In France, people say "Merci." I'll put that word on France. Now, choose a word from another country. Practice saying that word today when you show your gratitude.

Why It's Important
It is important for children to learn to express gratitude when it's appropriate. Learning how to say "thank you" in different languages shows that gratitude is felt and expressed all over the world.

the Optimistic classroom™ journal

LANGUAGE ARTS
Special Delivery

What to Do
Introduce the idea or the format of a friendly letter. Create a sample letter on chart paper for children to refer to, then have them compose a brief letter to someone they are grateful to have in their life. They can expand on one of the leaves from the gratitude tree they created. Younger children can draw a picture and a write a caption for the body of their letter.

What to Say
A letter has different parts. It has the date: May 5, 2012. It has a greeting: Dear Buster. Then it has a message. Finally, it has a closing: Love, Me. Today, let's write a letter to someone we are happy we know. You can pick one of your leaves off the gratitude tree and write to that person. Tell that person why you're grateful to have him or her in your life.

Why It's Important
If possible, arrange for children's letters to be delivered. Ask parents or caretakers to provide addresses and/or facilitate delivery. The gratitude will be doubled if the recipients respond; however, the point of the letters is to emphasize the importance of expressing gratitude without expecting a reward for doing so.

SOCIAL-EMOTIONAL LEARNING
Gratitude Stones

What to Do
Collect a number of smooth, small stones, at least one per child, and place them in a basket. Explain that these are gratitude stones and will help children remember to be thankful for things in their life. When children need a boost, they can take a stone, breathe deeply, and summon a happy memory. They can also use a stone to show gratitude to someone else.

What to Say
Hold a stone in your hand. Breathe deeply and think of a happy memory. Be grateful for the memory. Now bring your good feelings back into the class. Every day, hold a stone and remember things you're grateful for. To express gratitude to someone else in class, give that person a stone.

Why It's Important
Giving children tools to practice gratitude increases the likelihood they'll engage in the practice on their own. This cultivates mindful thinking and encourages children to regulate their behavior and take good emotional care of themselves.

Literature Link
Feeling Thankful
by Shelley Rotner and Sheila Kelly (2007). New York: Scholastic.

What does it mean to be thankful? It all depends on who you are and what is important to you. In this evocative photo essay a number of children express gratitude for things they can do and things they have—as well as for the special people in their lives.

More Books to Share

Baumann, Hans. (1995). *Thank You, Brother Bear.* New York: Scholastic.

Chessen, Betsey. (1998). *Thank You!* New York: Scholastic.

Pinkney, Jerry. (2009). *The Lion and the Mouse.* New York: Little, Brown.

the Optimistic classroom™ library

Performing Acts of
Kindness

What Are Acts of Kindness?
Good deeds… gestures of generosity…paying it forward. These expressions describe mindful action intended to help another living thing. Participating in such an action constitutes an act of kindness. Acts of kindness can be big or small, spontaneous or well planned.

Why Perform Acts of Kindness?
Think back to a time when someone helped you out unexpectedly or gave you a compliment. Memories like this have intense staying power (in fact, they may be part of a larger happy memory) and often remind us that we can act in the same way to help, encourage, or comfort someone else. Socially, acts of kindness cultivate shared happiness, build relationships, and give people a sense of connectedness to a group, community, or place—they are an excellent way to build a classroom community full of good will and optimism.

In this lesson, children plan several acts of kindness, which not only benefit the larger community but also help develop the neural networks that build their sense of compassion and empathy. The more people practice acts of kindness, the more likely they are to recognize and act on situations in which others are in need.

What Can You Expect to Observe?
"We like to say 'Helping hands belong to happy hearts.' My class was quick to notice not only how small acts of kindness made other children, parents, and teachers smile; it made them feel happy, too."
—Pre-K teacher

Linking to Brain Research

Our Brains Are Built for Compassion and Empathy

Being concerned about the welfare of others and understanding the feelings of those around us are basic skills for emotional intelligence. Compassion and empathy can be developed through mindfully practicing acts of kindness. As children develop compassion and empathy, they learn to recognize that their words and actions have an impact on others. This feeling of interconnectedness helps them reflect on their responses to the words and actions of others and better monitor and control their emotional responses. Practicing compassion and empathy builds the social and emotional competence that children need in order to be resilient and confident.

Brain research studies confirm the power of practicing kindness. Brain scans reveal that neural pathways involved in detecting emotions are dramatically strengthened in people with extensive, focused experiences in practicing compassion. Other studies have shown that our brains are rewarded for altruism with a release of dopamine during acts of kindness. We are hard-wired to feel good about doing good.

Scientists are discovering that compassion is an emotion as evolutionarily ancient as fear or anger. Brain scans of subjects feeling compassion while watching videos of strangers in despair and grief show activity not only in the higher brain's cortex but also in the hypothalamus and brain stem.

Clarify for the Class

"Our brain likes it when we're nice to others!" Explain that our brain works in a way that helps us want to understand how others feel and do kind things for others. When we act selflessly, our brain rewards us with good feelings.

Discuss: Think about a time when you were kind to someone. How did you feel afterward? How did you feel before that?

Getting Ready

Celebrating an Act of Kindness
At morning meeting, children may pass a stuffed bear to a peer who has done an act of kindness.

GOALS

- Children find three opportunities to show kindness and perform three acts of kindness.
- Children explore the benefits—for themselves and for others—of being kind.

MATERIALS

- chart paper

CREATING THE OPTIMISTIC CLASSROOM

Classroom Management Children learn what they live. Nurturing and modeling compassion and empathy in our classrooms reinforce our goals with children. Weave language that builds understanding and kindness into each day:

- Look at the expression on Vanessa's face. She looks sad. What can you do to make her feel better?

- Look at the smile on Miguel's face. His expression is so joyful. What did you say or do to make him happy?

- Those words must have been hurtful to you. Tell him calmly what he did to upset you and why you feel hurt.

- Thank you all for listening so well to the story I read you.

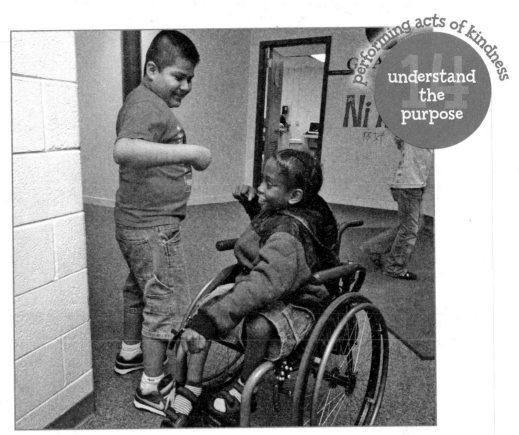

Fun-Filled Greeting
Daily acts of kindness
can include a special way
of saying hello, like this
fist-bump greeting.

MINDUP Warm-Up

Kindness Practice

On chart paper, create a web with the statement "Kindness counts!" in the center.
Ask children to chorally read the statement in the web. Share what this statement
means in your own life. Give an example of how you try to show kindness in your
daily routines with children.

*I greet each of you in the morning with a smile. I say, "Good morning! How are you
doing today?" I want you to know that I'm happy to see you. And, if I'm a little
grumpy, smiling makes me feel better. If you're feeling a little grumpy, then maybe
you'll feel better, too. Maybe you'll try smiling at someone else and asking how they
are. I'll write "smiling" on the web.*

Then ask children to share what kindness means in their own lives. Write their
responses on the web, paring them down as necessary.

PRE-K CORNER: Have younger children track each word in the sentence as you read
it aloud.

Discuss: How does kindness look? How does kindness sound? Tell about an act of
kindness you have seen at school. How did it make you feel?

Leading the Lesson

Performing Three Acts of Kindness

Engage

What to Do

Review the Kindness Counts! web you created in the warm-up. Then pose the following questions to broaden children's thinking about kindness and its role in their life:

- How much time does it take to be kind?

- Think about the feeling you have when someone is kind to you. How long does that feeling last?

- To be kind, do you need to spend any money?

- To be kind, do you need any special tools?

- Who or what in our world should we be kind to?

- How do you feel when you're kind?

- Does it matter whether anyone compliments us for being kind?

Work with children to develop a definition of kindness that includes the recognition that it is a mindful behavior, for example: "Kindness means caring about or helping someone or something. It is a mindful choice."

Why It's Important

Children realize that acting on kindness is a choice they can easily make and that kindness can take many forms. Share examples to expand their understanding of kindness arising from a single type of action, such as giving compliments to peers, to a range of acts that involves caring for people and other living things beyond the classroom, such as assisting others with special needs and taking care of plants and animals.

Explore

Relate kindness to gratitude, optimism, and perspective taking.

- Every day, we choose how we will treat others. Kindness is a mindful choice, just like gratitude and optimistic thinking. When we are kind, we are seeing someone else's point of view. We understand how that person is thinking and feeling.

Give an example of a time when children have shown kindness to you or others. Then ask children if they are ready to focus on making acts of kindness an even bigger part of their everyday lives. Tell children that all of you will perform at least three acts of kindness on the next day.

Review the acts of kindness to give children ideas of the types of actions they might undertake, such as smiling at and greeting someone they don't know well, giving someone a compliment, or acknowledging a person's hard work.

PRE-K CORNER: Add drawings to accompany each category on the Kindness Counts! web for younger children to use to record their acts of kindness.

Making connections among the concepts children have been learning and practicing may help them see how this positive, brain-building work all fits together. Older children may be able to grasp the role of perspective taking in acting kindly more easily than younger children; this is a concept that is important to emphasize and repeat.

From the Research

Children who are socially responsible, trust their classmates, and solve interpersonal problems in adaptive ways earn higher marks than those who do not.
(Wentzel, 1991)

Reflect

After children have completed their three acts of kindness, gather them to talk about their experiences. Ask them to select their most memorable act of kindness, make a sketch of what they did, and share it with a partner.

Call on volunteers to share. Help children understand that, as with being grateful and thinking optimistically, being kind to others makes us happier.

- Some scientists study the brain. They have learned that when people perform acts of kindness they become happier. We've learned that being optimistic thinkers and being grateful can help us be calmer and happier. These tools can help us think more clearly. Now we have learned another tool—being kind.

This reflection should guide children to understand:
- Helping others with our words and actions is a powerful way to improve our mood.

- Focusing on being kind brings happiness to others, and it also brings us happiness.

- Acts of kindness can boost our brain power and help us see the bigger picture in our lives.

MINDUP In the Real World

Career Connection

Many people have called kindness "the gift that costs nothing and rewards its giver with happiness and health." Performing acts of kindness boosts the positive energy of both the one who gives and the one who receives. Scientists are studying what happens to your brain when it's focused on kindness. In this way, neuroscience meets up with being a "good person." Is that surprising?

Discuss: Why is doing something nice for another person a gift you give yourself? Think of a way an act of kindness has helped someone else learn or feel part of the class community.

Once a Day

Reach out professionally and personally to colleagues. Share a creative teaching tip, remember a birthday, and build a more supportive work environment.

Connecting to the Curriculum

Performing acts of kindness supports children's connection to their own learning process and to the content areas and literature.

Journal Writing

Encourage children to reflect on what they've learned about doing kind actions and to record questions to explore at another time. They may also enjoy responding to these prompts:

- Start a Kindness Counts! page in your journal. Write down or draw sketches of acts of kindness that you do or that others do for you.

- Practice smiling more today and notice what happens. Then write a poem about what a powerful tool a smile is.

- Create a list of acts of kindness that everyone in your class can practice every day.

- **Pre-K & Kindergarten:** Have children draw a picture of someone who is sad or upset. Ask them what the person says and write it in a speech balloon. Then have children draw a picture of themselves being kind to the person. Record their dialogue in a speech balloon.

SCIENCE
Be Kind to Living Things

What to Do
Young children learn the importance of kindness by focusing on taking care of the environment and the plants and animals in it. Show them how to construct a bird feeder and hang it outside your window: Attach a pipe cleaner to the top of a pinecone. Spread peanut butter or shortening on the pine cone and roll it in birdseed. Set aside time every day to observe the kinds of birds that visit the feeder.

What to Say
Do any of you have bird feeders at home? Sometimes, especially in the winter, there are not enough seeds in nature for birds to eat. Filling a bird feeder with birdseed and hanging it can help them get enough to eat. Let's watch the birds that visit the feeder that we made and hung outside. What kinds of birds do you see?

Why It's Important
Children learn that kindness extends not only to people but also to plants, animals, and the environment. Consider other nature-themed science projects, such as observing spiders and insects without disrupting or destroying their habitats, picking up litter, and so on.

MATH
Kindness Paper Chain

What to Do
Set out 1-inch strips of construction paper in four different colors. As children perform acts of kindness, have them write or sketch the deed on a strip according to a color code, then deposit the strips in a container. Once a week, review the contents and graph the data. Staple the strips into an ever-growing chain.

What to Say
Each time you do a kind deed, write it or draw it on a strip of paper. Then put the paper into this container. Use different colors for different deeds: RED is for kind deeds you do for people outside of school; YELLOW is for kind deeds you do for someone you don't know well; BLUE is for kind deeds you do at school; GREEN is for kind deeds you do for the environment.

Why It's Important
Seeing their deeds recorded in a graph and watching their paper chain grow provide a concrete representation of their many kind acts.

the Optimistic classroom™ journal

LANGUAGE ARTS
A Class-ic Book of Kindness

What to Do
Collect children's personal narratives about acts of kindness done for them or that they've done for others. Compile them into a class Book of Kindness. Depending upon their level, children may write, draw, or dictate their narratives. Encourage them to explore how the acts of kindness made them and others feel and whether the act was easy or challenging to perform.

What to Say
Think about an act of kindness you've done or that someone has done for you. How did it feel to treat someone kindly? Or how did it feel to be treated kindly? Was your act of kindness easy to do? Or was it hard? Write about it or draw a picture of it or tell me about it. I'll collect your pages into a class Kindness Book for your families and friends and other classes to enjoy.

Why It's Important
Contemplating the ease or difficulty of an act of kindness will give children a greater sense of how mindful a behavior it is. Some acts can be incorporated easily into day-to-day life, while other acts require more time, effort, and thought.

SOCIAL-EMOTIONAL LEARNING
Kindness Banners

What to Do
Ask children to work in pairs and groups of three to create kindness banners to display in the classroom and around school. Have them decide on a slogan to write on the banner—it can be as simple as "Be Kind!" —and then illustrate it with an example of a kind act. Invite other classes to the unveiling of the banners.

What to Say
Let's create Kindness Banners to hang around the school. Work with your team. Think of a slogan for your banner. What do you want to say about doing kind acts? Then draw a picture of someone doing a kind act. When we hang up the banner, you can say a few words about how it feels to be kind.

Why It's Important
Sharing their knowledge with other classes will help develop children's vocabulary and oral skills. Working together on the banner will also help prepare children for their group effort in Lesson 15.

Literature Link
Crazy Hair Day
by Barney Saltzberg
(2003). New York: Scholastic.

Stanley is all ready for Crazy Hair Day. But when he arrives at school it turns out that today is actually School Picture Day. Crazy Hair Day is next week! Stanley is horrified until an act of kindness from his class helps him fit right in.

Help children connect the events in this funny story with creative ways in which they can demonstrate kindness in real life.

More Books to Share

Lewin, Ted. (1999). *Nilo and the Tortoise*. New York: Scholastic.

Murphy, Mary. (2004). *How Kind!* New York: Walker.

Williams, Vera B. (1982). *A Chair for My Mother*. New York: Scholastic.

the Optimistic classroom™ library

Taking Mindful Action in the **World**

What Are Mindful Actions?

Whether they involve one or many individuals, mindful actions are purposefully planned activities that create a healthier, happier world and set a precedent for other people to follow. You might say that mindful actions take acts of kindness to the world beyond the classroom.

Why Go Beyond the Classroom?

At this point in their MindUp learning journey, children have a range of optimism-building strategies to call on. They are beginning to feel confident in their ability to monitor and nurture themselves and to be receptive to the perspectives and needs of others. They are ready to expand their kindness practice to make a bigger "ripple effect" in their world.

In this culminating lesson, children work together to select, plan, and execute a group act of kindness for the school, larger community, or the world. Through actions like this, children are able to see themselves as part of a larger community— they glimpse the big picture of the world around them, and link their own peace of mind to a more generalized sense of peace. Their role as active participants in building that community fosters a sense of comfort, belonging, and optimism and increases their desire to make thoughtful, ethical decisions both independently and with others.

What Can You Expect to Observe?

"I was concerned about figuring out all the logistics for our school recycling project, but my students were so motivated to make their project successful that they came up with inventive solutions for sharing the work and scheduling collection times. What a fantastic opportunity for them to see how planning with your PFC can help make a big idea work!" —Second-grade teacher

Linking to Brain Research

Mirror Neurons: Kindness Is Contagious!

Research on mirror neurons is helping us understand the power of social interactions and connections. Mirror neurons are a kind of brain nerve cell that allows the brain to imitate the actions of others, and also to feel the emotions experienced by others. Our pain receptors flinch (as does our body) when we see someone stub a toe. Our amygdala relaxes when we see a mother gently rocking her baby. The neural pathways associated with specific emotions such as pain, joy, and fear are activated when we see a face expressing that emotion.

When a group works together in a positive way—specifically, through altruism—feelings of kindness, enhanced levels of dopamine, and opportunities for activating the neural pathways of pleasure and reward multiply. This makes kindness "contagious." Recent studies show that individuals who belong to social groups that focus on kindness and altruism have higher levels of dopamine, and more empathy and compassion. As we engage in acts of kindness and are emotionally rewarded for it, our need to be kind becomes a deciding factor in our choice of words and actions.

Mirror neurons in certain regions of the brain activate in an identical manner both during an emotional experience and when seeing someone else have that emotional experience.

Clarify for the Class

Explain that being concerned about the feelings of others teaches our brains to read emotions. Provide children with some dramatic images—both happy and sad. Ask them to look at the images and share what they think the people in them are most likely feeling.

Discuss: How do you think the people in the pictures feel? Do you think they feel happy, sad, or lonely? How do the pictures make you feel?

Getting Ready

Who Wants to Help?
Children volunteer to help with tasks to complete their fund-raising project.

GOALS

- Children work cooperatively to plan and perform an act of kindness for the school or the larger community.
- Children reflect on their feelings as they make a positive difference through kind actions.

MATERIALS

- chart paper
- Mindful Action Planner (p. 158)

CREATING THE OPTIMISTIC CLASSROOM

Brain-Inspired Instruction When we consciously cultivate a sense of community in our classroom and make it a place full of opportunities for low-risk but purposeful and positive actions, the result is that all children—regardless of ability, socio-economic, or maturity level—become more socially and emotionally competent. An amygdala-friendly environment allows children to think more optimistically and to look outward for opportunities to positively interact with others. Start a ripple of kindness in your classroom by:

- acknowledging the acts of kindness you see among children
- treating children with the same kindness you hope to see them exhibit

Kind Acts for Our School
Weekly projects like collecting
and sorting recycling provide
young children with regular
opportunities to contribute to
the larger school community.

MINDUP Warm-Up

Introducing Mindful Action Practice

Gather children in a circle. Ask them to close their eyes and practice mindful
breathing. Then relate the following scenario to help them see the power of
group action:

*Imagine we are all sitting in the dark. It is completely dark. One of us has a
flashlight. The flashlight helps, but it only gives a small amount of light. Now
imagine that each of us has a flashlight. Everyone turn on your flashlight. See how
light it is? It doesn't seem dark at all. An act of kindness is like a flashlight. We know
that one person can make a difference by being kind. Think what we can do when
we work together to do an act of kindness!*

Discuss: What would happen if each of us pointed our flashlight at a different
point? What would happen if we all decided to point our flashlight at the same point
at the same time?

Leading the Lesson

Practicing Mindful Action Together

Engage

Explore

What to Do

Briefly review the warm-up with children. Connect it to the power of unified group action they will do in this lesson.

Ask children to brainstorm some mindful acts of kindness that would make a difference for a lot of people—a class in your school, a group in the community, or the whole school or community.

- Each of us has been practicing acts of kindness. Now let's work together to help someone or something.

- We could help another class in our school, a group in our community, or the entire school or community.

- Share your ideas with a partner.

List children's ideas on chart paper. Guide them toward projects you can help them manage, such as picking up litter on a playground, interacting with a senior citizens group, donating gently used toys to a shelter, or writing thank-you cards to local police and firefighters. Help children narrow the list to three and then have them vote on one.

Engage children in planning their group's act of kindness. (Note that the action may take place over the course of several days or weeks.) Display the Mindful Action Planner activity sheet and complete it with their help, or create your own. Encourage children's participation by allowing them to:

- choose the day, time, or time frame for preparations for the action and the action itself

- list and undertake preparations for the action

- tell others about the plan

- decide upon any follow-up activities, such as writing thank-you notes to adult helpers

Revisit the Mindful Action Planner frequently so that children can discuss their progress and what they still need to do. Before the day of the action, confirm arrangements and preparations and enlist the help of families to ensure its success.

On the day of the action, repeat the warm-up activity to help children focus on the power of working together.

Why It's Important

Brainstorming ideas and then discussing and voting on them helps children become invested in the group action. You may need to offer input about the needs that exist in your community. (There are several websites devoted to suggestions for group acts of kindness.)

Children learn to work together to plan and implement the steps necessary for a successful project. To keep children engaged and focused, provide structure in organizing the planning. Plan different tasks over the course of several days in short, focused periods. Provide a helpful visual reminder by posting a calendar and marking key dates on it. Color-code tasks to help children organize themselves.

Reflect

After their mindful action, ask children to share their
experiences and thoughts about their participation.

- How did you feel while we worked together
  on our plan?

- How do you feel now about our mindful action?

- What did you notice about the way everyone
  worked together?

- Would you like to do more group acts of
  kindness in the future? Why?

Point out to children that this lesson has given
them another chance to make mindful choices and
to make their brain healthier.

- We focused on understanding and helping
  other people. That made us feel happier.
  Our amygdala was calm. Our PFC was more
  aware. Our hippocampus stored our good
  memories about our act of kindness.

By working together as a group, children realize
that they can accomplish great things and build
community. They also get the "big picture" of the
world around them—and see how they fit into it.

MINDUP
In the Real World

Career Connection

One for one—that's not only the
philosophy behind TOMS shoes, founded
by Blake Mycoskie, but also its business
model. For every pair of shoes this
innovative company sells, it donates a
new pair to a child in need. So when you
buy a pair of TOMS shoes, you're not just
buying for yourself, you're also putting
shoes on the feet of a child without. Why
shoes? Because in developing countries
many diseases are soil-transmitted—they
penetrate the skin through bare feet. Also,
shoes protect feet from cuts and sores and
enable children to go to school.

Discuss: How is "one for one" like
sharing with a friend? Think of a time
when sharing food or some other item
helped both you and your friend.

Once a Day

Consider how teaching can be a "one
for one" service. How can you create
situations in which your teaching is
absorbed by students and then passed
along to others in the school (e.g., buddy
teaching with younger students)?

Connecting to the Curriculum

Taking mindful action supports children's connection to their own learning process and to the content areas and literature.

Journal Writing

Encourage children to reflect on what they've learned about taking mindful action and to record questions to explore at another time. They may also enjoy responding to these prompts:

- How can you help make your community even better? Write a letter to your friends and ask them to help you.

- Imagine that you are a plant or an animal that has been protected by a group of people. Draw a picture of the plant or animal. Add a thought balloon. Write about how you were helped.

- Celebrate taking mindful action in your community. Design a Mindful Action badge to give to people who help.

- **Pre-K & Kindergarten:** Ask younger children to draw a picture showing themselves working in a group to help the community—picking up litter, digging holes for plants or watering them, singing to senior citizens, and so on.

LANGUAGE ARTS/ART
T-Shirt for a Cause

What to Do
If you have any T-shirts you've bought to support a cause, bring them in to show children. Explain that many charities hold events, such as walks and runs or festivals, and sell T-shirts to raise money. Have children design their own special T-shirt to commemorate their mindful action project.

What to Say
Some groups hold activities to raise money for a good cause. A group might put on a walk or a run. Often, the people who participate buy a T-shirt. The T-shirt celebrates the event. Today, we're going to design our own T-shirt to celebrate our mindful action project. Think of a picture and any words that will describe our project.

Why It's Important
Children will have a limited space to display their graphic, so they'll have to distill their experience into something meaningful to them and to others who may not be familiar with the cause. They'll also get to see which elements of their designs they have in common and which elements portray their own unique response to the experience.

MATH
We Count

What to Do
Ask children to imagine that counters are pennies. Give one counter to each child and group children in pairs. Have partners count their money: 1 cent, 2 cents. Record the amount on the board or chart paper. Then form groups of four. Again, count and record. Continue to double the size of the groups and record the amounts.

What to Say
Each of you has one counter. Pretend it is one cent. Work with a partner. Combine your counters. How many cents do you have? Now, two pairs work together. Combine your counters and count your cents. What happens to the money? What happens when more people work together?

Why It's Important
Using counters to represent pennies allows children to see the cumulative impact of people combining their forces to work together. The act of combining and counting their counters reinforces the mathematical concepts of adding on and patterns.

the Optimistic classroom™ journal

SCIENCE
Every Day Is Earth Day

What to Do

Show kindness to the earth by consciously conserving resources. Explain where the trash in your community goes. Then have children help you weigh the amount of trash they produce in a day. You can use a bathroom scale, but be sure to deduct its weight from the total. Talk about strategies for reducing the amount of trash the class produces. After implementing the strategies for a week, weigh your trash again.

What to Say

Our trash goes into a landfill. The city digs a huge hole. Our trash goes there and is covered up. The more trash we create, the more landfills we need. How much trash do you think we produce every day? Let's weigh our trash to find out. How do you think we can cut down on the number of things we throw away? We'll try some of those ideas and then weigh our trash again.

Why It's Important

Weighing the trash will help children become more mindful of the items they throw away each day. They may become inspired to work together to create a recycling program for the school or a composting program for the cafeteria.

SOCIAL-EMOTIONAL LEARNING
What Can We Do Next?

What to Do

Keep your group of children motivated to continue initiating mindful actions. Establish a mindful-action center in your classroom. Stock it with information on different needs in the school and community, the ideas that children generated in the lesson, a book documenting their mindful action project, and picture books. Set out a box for children's suggestions for future projects.

What to Say

Let's keep our mindful action going! Our mindful-action center will help us do that. Here is a list of places that may need our help. Here is our list of ideas for projects. This book is about the project we did together. When you have an idea for a new mindful action project, write it down and put it here.

Why It's Important

Establishing a mindful-action center shows children that working together to help others can be ongoing. The materials in the center give them the tools to take responsibility for future projects and help them celebrate their successes.

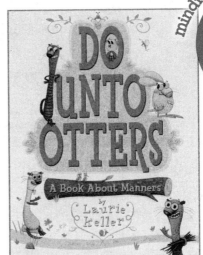

Literature Link
Do Unto Otters

by Laurie Keller
(2009). New York: Scholastic.

This wacky guide to manners is based on the Golden Rule. Rabbit is worried when he discovers that a family of otters is moving in next door. How is he supposed to treat them? A wise friend reminds him that all he has to do is treat the otters as he, himself, would like to be treated.

Encourage children to explore the clever cartoon art to fully appreciate the story.

More Books to Share

Christelow, Eileen. (1993). *The Five Dog Night.* New York: Clarion.

Readman, Jo. (2007). *George Saves the Earth by Lunchtime.* London: Transworld Publishers.

Rylant, Cynthia. (1996). *The Bookshop Dog.* (1996). New York: Blue Sky Press.

the Optimistic classroom™ library

Brain Power!

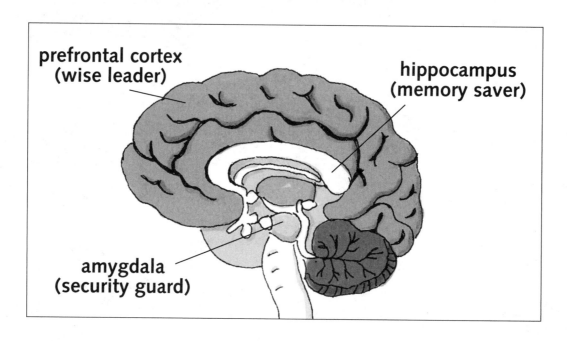

prefrontal cortex
(wise leader)

hippocampus
(memory saver)

amygdala
(security guard)

What does each part of the brain do? Draw a line to match.

1. amygdala

a. helps us make good decisions

2. prefrontal cortex

b. helps us learn and remember

3. hippocampus

c. helps protect us

Name _____

Date _____

Mindful or Unmindful?

Mindful	Unmindful
Listening to someone read a story and being able to retell it	Not speaking to someone because he or she has not spoken to you
Practicing a new skill during a sports practice or music lesson until you feel your body improving	Crossing the street without looking both ways
Keeping your voice quiet when other people are reading	Trying to do too many things at the same time
Tasting a new food, even if it looks different from anything you've eaten	Leaving your shoes in the middle of the living room
Helping someone in need	Daydreaming or "tuning out" to what is happening around you
Listening to someone and not speaking until they are finished	Ignoring a classmate who wants to join your game or group

Name _____

Date _____

Sounds & Scents

Mindfully listen to the mystery sound or smell the mystery scent. Describe what you notice. Then make a guess.

What I Noticed	My Guess
1.	
2.	
3.	
4.	

Name _____

Date _____

Sensory Web

What are you observing? Tell what it is or draw a picture of it in the middle.
Use your senses. Draw or write what you notice in the other spaces.

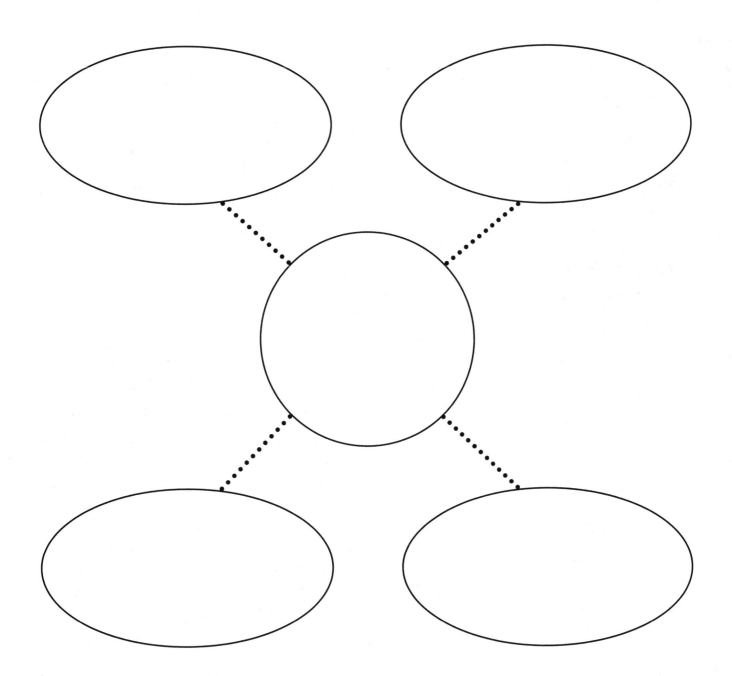

Name _____

Date _____

Character Feelings

Story Title: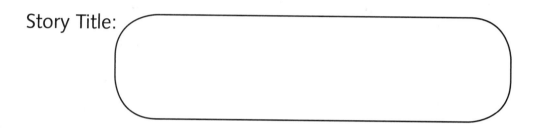

What happened in the story?
Draw an important event, or write about it.

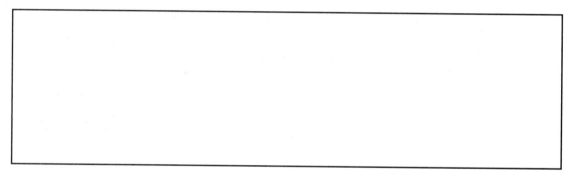

How did the character feel?
Draw a picture.

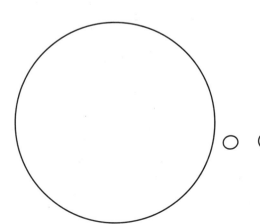

What did the character think?
Write in the thought balloon.

Name _____

Date _____

Optimistic/Pessimistic Thoughts

What is your problem?

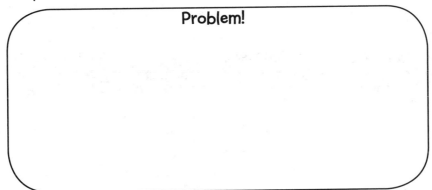

Problem!

What does the optimistic thinker say?

What does the pessimistic thinker say?

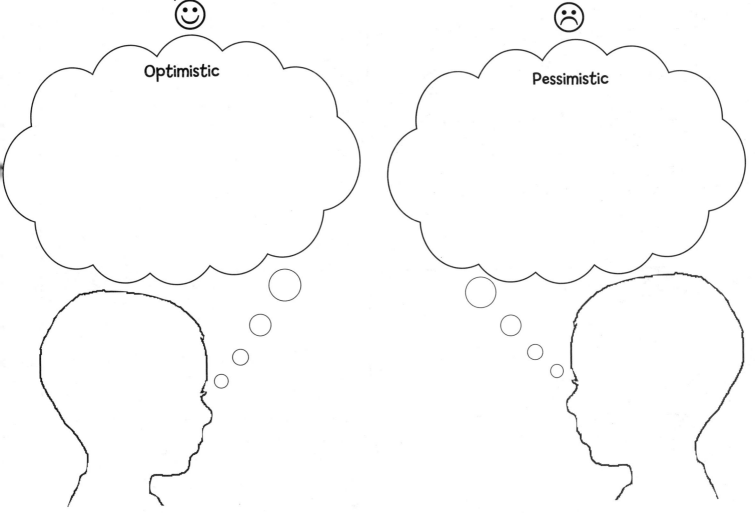

Optimistic

Pessimistic

Name _____

Date _____

Mindful Action Planner

Event _____   Event Date _____

Task	Things We Need
1. ☐	
2. ☐	
3. ☐	
4. ☐	

Glossary

adrenal glands
organs located on the kidneys, responsible for releasing stress hormones such as cortisol and adrenaline (epinephrine)

amygdala
an almond-shaped structure which is a part of the limbic system that encodes emotional messages for long-term storage in the brain

brain stem
a brain part, comprising midbrain, pons, and medulla oblongata, which receives sensory input and monitors vital functions such as heartbeat, body temperature, and digestion. The RAS is located in the brain stem

Core Practice
deep belly breathing that relies on mindful, focused attention; it is recommended that the core practice be done three times each day for a few minutes—depending on the age of the student

cortisol (hydrocortisone)
a hormone produced by the adrenal gland in response to stress or to a low level of blood glucocorticoids, the primary functions of which are to increase blood sugar, suppress the immune system, and aid in fat, protein and carbohydrate metabolism

dopamine
a neurotransmitter that produces feelings of pleasure when released by the brain reward system; has multiple functions depending on where in the brain it acts

endorphin
a neurotransmitter with properties similar to opiates that are important for pain reduction and the creation of pleasant and euphoric feelings

epinephrine (adrenalin)
a hormone secreted by the adrenal glands

executive function
mental management that includes higher-order skills dependent upon the thinker's ability to reflect before reacting: evaluating information, organizing, focusing attention, prioritizing, planning, and problem solving

fight, flight, or freeze response
neurophysiological mechanism of the sympathetic nervous system in response to real or perceived threat

glutamate
the most common excitatory neurotransmitter in the brain

hippocampus
a brain structure that compares new learning to past learning and encodes information from working memory to long-term storage.

hypothalamus
a brain structure at the base of the limbic area that regulates body functions in response to internal and external stimuli, controls the pituitary

limbic system
the collection of cortical and subcortical structures, including amygdala and hippocampus, situated at the base of the cerebrum that control emotions, motivations, and other behaviors, and are important for memory functions.

mindful attention
focused awareness; purposeful, nonjudgmental attentiveness

mindfulness
state of being in touch with and aware of the present moment in a nonjudgmental way. Mindfulness is an approach used by mental health professionals as a kind of therapy that helps people suffering from difficulties such as anxiety and depression.

mirror neuron
a neuron that responds when one performs a certain action or when one observes the same action performed by another. Thus, the neuron "mirrors" the behavior of the other, as though the observer were performing the action.

neural pathway
usually, a series of nerve bundles that connect relatively distant areas of the brain or nervous system

neuron
a nerve cell, which is a cell specialized for excitability and conductivity, composed of an axon, a soma, and dendrites. (All neurons have one soma and one axon; some neurons have many dendrites and others have none.)

neuroplasticity
the brain's lifelong ability to reorganize neural networks as a result of new or repeated experiences

neuroscience
an interdisciplinary science focused on the brain and nervous system and closely associated other disciplines such as psychology, mathematics, physics, philosophy, and medicine

neurotransmitter
one of many chemicals that transmit signals across a synaptic gap from one neuron to another.

norepinephrine
a neurotransmitter and a hormone that is part of the fight, flight, or freeze response. In the brain, norepinephrine acts as a neurotransmitter—usually excitatory, sometimes inhibitory—to regulate normal brain processes.

positive psychology
scientific study of the strengths and virtues that enable individuals and communities to thrive. (Understanding positive emotions entails the study of contentment with the past, happiness in the present, and hope for the future. Understanding positive individual traits consists of the study of the strengths and virtues, such as the capacity for love and work, courage, compassion, resilience, creativity, curiosity, integrity, self-knowledge, moderation, self-control, and wisdom. Understanding positive institutions entails the study of the strengths that foster better communities, such as justice, responsibility, civility, parenting, nurturance, work ethic, leadership, teamwork, purpose, and tolerance.)

prefrontal cortex
a part of the brain that dominates the frontal lobe, implicated in executive function, planning complex cognitive behavior, personality expression, decision-making and moderating correct social behavior and considered to be orchestration of thoughts and actions in accordance with internal goals.

reticular activating system (RAS)
a dense formation of neurons and fibers in the brain stem that controls major body functions and mediates various levels of brain response

social-emotional learning (SEL)
the process of developing the fundamental life skills needed to effectively and ethically handle ourselves, our relationships, and our work

synapse
the microscopic gap between the axon of one neuron and the dendrite of another, that serves to connect neurons. Synapses connect them functionally, not physically, enabling neurons to communicate by passing signals between them.

thalamus
receives and integrates all incoming sensory information, except smell, and directs it to other areas of the cortex for additional processing.

unmindfulness
lack of awareness; uncontrolled actions, emotions, or thoughts

Resource List

Allyn, P., Margolies, J. & McNalley, K. (2010). *The Great Eight: Management strategies for the reading and writing classroom.* New York: Scholastic.

Alston, L. (2007). *Why we teach: Learning, laughter, love, and the power to transform lives.* New York: Scholastic.

Ashby, C. R., Thanos, P. K., Katana, J. M., Michaelides, E. L., Gardner, C. A. & Heidbreder, N. D. (1999). The selective dopamine antagonist. *Pharmacology, Biochemistry and Behavior.*

Brown, K. W. & Ryan, R. M. (2003). The benefits of being present: Mindfulness and its role in psychological well-being. *Journal of Personality and Social Psychology*, 84(4), 822–848.

Caprara, G. V., Barbanelli, C., Pastorelli, C., Bandura, A. & Zimbardo, P. G. (2000). Prosocial foundations of children's academic achievement. *Psychological Science, 11*: 302–306.

Collaborative for Academic, Social, and Emotional Learning (CASEL). (2010). Retrieved from: http://www.casel.org/basics/skills.php.

Diamond, A. (2009). *SoundSeen: In the room with Adele Diamond.* NPR. November 19, 2009. Retrieved from: http://being.publicradio.org/programs/2009/learning-doing-being.

Durlak, J. A., Weissberg, R. P., Dymnicki, A. B., Taylor, R. D. & Schellinger, K. B. (2011). Enhancing students' social and emotional development promotes success in school: Results of a meta-analysis. *Child Development.*

Galvan, A., Hare, T., Parra, C., Penn, J., Voss, H., Glover, G. & Casey, B. (2006). Earlier development of the accumbens relative to orbitofrontal cortex might underlie risk-taking behavior in adolescents. *Journal of Neuroscience.* 26(25), 6885-6892.

Greenberg, M.T., Weissberg, R.P., Utne O'Brien, M., Zins, J.E., Fredericks, L., Resnik, H. & Elias, M.J. (2003). Enhancing school-based prevention and youth development through coordinated social, emotional, and academic learning. *American Psychologist, 58*, 466-474.

Greenland, S. K. (2010). *The Mindful Child: How to Help Your Kid Manage Stress and Become Happier, Kinder, and More Compassionate.* New York: Simon & Schuster, Inc.

Goleman, D. (2008). Emotional intelligence. Retrieved from: http://danielgoleman.info/topics/emotional-intelligence.

Iidaka, T., Anderson N., Kapur, S., Cabeza R. & Craik, F. (2000). The effect of divided attention on encoding and retrieval in episodic memory revealed by positron emission tomography. *Journal of Cognitive Neuroscience*, 12(2). 267–280.

Jensen, E. (2009). *Teaching with poverty in mind: What being poor does to kids' brains and what schools can do about it.* Alexandria, VA: ASCD.

Jensen, E. (2003). *Tools for engagement.* Thousand Oaks, CA.: Corwin Press.

Kann, L., Kinchen, S. A. Williams, B. I., Ross, J. G., Lowry, R., Grunbaum, J. A. & Kolbe, L. J. (2000). Youth risk behavior surveillance in United States, 1999. Centers for Disease Control MMWR Surveillance Summaries, 49(SS-5), 1–96.

Kato, N. & McEwen, B. (2003). Neuromechanisms of emotions and memory. *Neuroendocrinology*, 11, 03. 54–58.

Lutz, A., Dunne, J. D., & Davidson, R. J. (2007). Meditation and the neuroscience of consciousness: An introduction. In Zelazo, P., Moscovitch, M., & Thompson, E. (Eds.), *The Cambridge Handbook of Consciousness* (499–554). Cambridge, UK: Cambridge University Press.

McCullough, M. E., Kilpatrick, S. D., Emmons, R. A. & Larson, D. B. (2001). Is gratitude a moral affect? *Psychological Bulletin*, 127, 249–266.

Pascual-Leone, A. Amedi, A., Fregni, F. & Merabet, L. B. (2005). The plastic human brain cortext. *Annual Review of Neuroscience*, 28, 377-401.

Pawlak, R., Magarinos, A. M., Melchor, J., McEwen, B. & Strickland, S. (February 2003). Tissue plasminogen activator in the amygdala is critical for stress-induced anxiety-like behavior. *Nature Neuroscience*, 168–174.

Payton, J. Weissberg, R.P., Dulak, J.A., Dymnicki, A.B. Taylor, R.D., Schellinger, K.B. & Pachan, M. (2008). The positive impact of social and emotional learning for kindergarten to eighth-grade students. Findings from three scientific reviews. Chicago, IL: Collaborative for Academic, Social, and Emotional Learning. Retrieved from: www.casel.org or www.lpfch.org/sel.

Posner, M. I. & Patoine, B. (2009). How Arts Training Improves Attention and Cognition. The Dana Foundation. Available: http://www.dana.org/news/cerebrum/detail.aspx?id=23206.

Ratey, J. J. (2008). *Spark: The revolutionary new science of exercise and the brain.* New York: Little, Brown & Co.

Revising the rules of perception, retrieved from http://news.vanderbilt.edu/2010/07/binocularvisio, posted 7/29/10.

Schonert-Reichl, K. A., & Lawlor, M. S. (2010). The effects of a mindfulness-based education program on pre- and early adolescents' well-being and social and emotional competence. *Mindfulness, 1*, 137–151.

Schonert-Reichl, Kimberly A. (2008). Effectiveness of the Mindfulness Education (ME) Program: Research Summary, 2005-2008. Retrieved from: http://www.thehawnfoundation.org/.../2007/.../summary-of-the-effectiveness-of-the-me-program_april2009ksrfinal1.pdf.

Shadmehr, R. & Holcomb, H. (1997). Neural correlates of motor memory consolidation. *Science 277*: 821.

Tatum, A. (2009). *Reading for their life: Rebuilding the textual lineages of African-American adolescent males.* Portsmouth, NH: Heinemann

Wentzel, K. R. (1991). Social competence at school: Relation between social responsibility and academic achievement. *Review of Educational Research*, 61(1), 1–24.

Willis, J. (2006). *Research-based Strategies to Ignite Student Learning: Insights from a Neurologist and Classroom Teacher.* Danvers, MA: Association for Supervision and Curriculum Development.

Willis, J. (2008). *How Your Child Learns Best: Brain-Friendly Strategies You Can Use to Ignite Your Child's Learning and Increase School Success.* Naperville, IL: Sourcebooks.